GUERRILLA PROJECT MANAGEMENT

GUERRILLA PROJECT MANAGEMENT

Kenneth T. Hanley
M. Eng. (Project Management)

MANAGEMENTCONCEPTS

ʃʃʃ
MANAGEMENTCONCEPTS

8230 Leesburg Pike, Suite 800
Vienna, VA 22182
(703) 790-9595
Fax: (703) 790-1371
www.managementconcepts.com

Printed in the United States of America

Library of Congress Cataloging-in-Publication Data

Hanley, Kenneth T.

   Guerilla project management / Kenneth T. Hanley.
      p. cm.
   ISBN 978-1-56726-294-0
1. Project management. I. Title.
HD69.P75H3573 2011
658.4′04–dc22

                                                     2010037429

10   9   8   7   6   5   4   3   2   1

About the Author

Ken Hanley has been a program management director and principal in a number of large organizations, including KPMG and BearingPoint. He focuses on the effective management of large and complex programs, IT project management, strategic portfolio management, establishing and operating project management offices, and other advanced project management practices. He also helps save troubled projects in a number of industries by working with and mentoring project managers.

Ken has a roster of international clients and extensive experience with projects ranging from offshore energy exploration and mining to health-care initiatives to international export market development to the Vancouver 2010 Winter Olympic Games.

Ken regularly lectures on effective leadership, organization, and program and project management. He has taught for the graduate management and engineering programs at the University of Calgary and has been guest lecturer for the Queen's MBA in Science and Technology, Royal Roads University, and the Executive MBA program at the University of Alberta.

A recognized project management expert, Ken is in demand as a speaker at project management conferences around the world. He was nominated for the Southern Alberta Project Management Institute's 2005 Distinguished Contribution Award.

He has a master's degree in Engineering (Project Management) from the University of Calgary.

To Dr. Francis Hartman, the father of SMART Project Management™—upon which much that follows is based—and the man who taught us the really important stuff.

CONTENTS

PREFACE

As we've paid increasing attention to project management practices over the last few years, we've formalized and "technocratized" the world of projects by setting up project management offices, cranking out Gantt charts and work breakdown structures, installing project management software, compressing critical paths, and comparing the actual cost of work performed against the budgeted cost of work performed. We're focusing more on project management than we ever have before, but we're still not making the progress we should be. And that's because we're focused mostly on *project mechanics* and not nearly enough on what really does and doesn't make projects work—the "looser" pieces, the people pieces, the tuning-into-the-project-environment pieces.

Sure, we're making progress on "keeping it tight"—project managers (PMs) are more educated than ever before; the number of Project Management Professionals (PMPs) is growing; and there's a greater emphasis on project disciplines. But we've got some work to do when it comes to keeping it *loose*. We seem to have forgotten—or never developed—the critical skills needed to keep our projects light, fast, and flexible.

Effective project management *doesn't* mean a slavish adherence to a mechanical set of practices. The repeated application of the same PM "stuff" the same way for every project quickly reveals the flaws in that approach: It falters because projects differ not just by size, but also by *complexity*, as reflected in the degree of risk and uncertainty inherent in them and in the number and variety of stakeholders involved with them.

Competencies, Processes, and Tools (CPTs)

Project management competencies—the Cs—are much more important than project management processes—the Ps—which in turn, are much more important than the project management tools—the Ts. Therefore, this book focuses on competencies first, processes where necessary to support competencies, and tools if (and only if) they're required to support processes. (And by tools, I mean project management software in general.)

PMs first need to develop and then master the *fundamental competencies* of effective project management. They need to know how to manage stakeholders effectively, assess risk accurately, and look for and get agreement on the objective measures of project success, for example, before they bring processes and tools to bear.

The *competency* associated with effectively managing and communicating with stakeholders, for example, can be supported by the stakeholder breakdown process (see Chapter 11), but it certainly doesn't require a software *tool*. Competent risk assessors may use the impact and probability assessment *process* (see Chapter 17) to communicate the risks that they're seeing and how they're seeing them from an impact and probability perspective, but that doesn't require a software tool either. And PMs can establish workable measures of success for a project by using the Three Key Questions (see Chapter 9), but they don't need PM software to manage against them. Tools don't even come into the picture until far into project planning—if they're required at all—and they're really the last and the least important element of the Cs, Ps, and Ts.

Effective project management should *never* start with PM software. But I'll bet you know a PM or two who wants to grab on to MS Project right from the start, to build a Gantt chart or a project evaluation and review technique (PERT) chart before, honestly, they understand what the project they're cramming into the software is *really all about*. Some PMs take erroneous comfort in loading their project data into a PM tool, and they mistakenly assume that they now have a proxy for control. ("I have a Gantt chart... now we're getting somewhere.") This isn't true: What these PMs are really doing is acting out the old saying, "If your only tool is a hammer, every problem looks like a nail."

But we know better. We know that starting with a tool is *never* a good idea, and PM tools, in fact, aren't even that important to a successful project. They're so unimportant, in fact, that you won't find them discussed in this book.

Flexibility

I don't care what your manuals or textbooks say. The competencies, processes, and tools you bring to bear on a project *shouldn't* be the same every time. Instead, the CPTs you choose should depend entirely on the kind of project you're dealing with. Notice that I said *kind of project*, not *size of project*; choosing an approach to managing a project based simply on its size (which is often expressed as its expected cost) is overly simplistic and often less than useful.

To illustrate: Which project is "bigger" and more complicated to manage—one expected to cost $100 million or one expected to cost $25 million? What if I said that the $100 million project was about replacing an old pipeline with new pipe and that $80 million of its $100 million budget was for the purchase and installation of standard steel pipe on the preexisting pipeline right-of-way? And then what if I told you that the $25 million project was all about developing facial recognition software for the U.S. Department of Homeland Security? The pipeline project is certainly "bigger" than the software project in terms of cost, but it's also much less complex, and it would be an amateur's error—an error that's made all the time—to assume that the CPTs the PM should bring to the table should be more comprehensive for the "bigger" project.

Size alone, then (and even more certainly, cost), is not a particularly good criterion by which to decide on the right CPTs. But complexity is. What *are* the best criteria to help determine a project's level of complexity? How about risk? How risky is this project? How much *don't* you know going in? Have you and your team ever done a project like this before? Does the amount of risk involved suggest what CPTs you might use and to what extent? It should.

How about uncertainty? Are you so experienced with what you're doing this time that your early estimates can be considered "tight" and dependable based on previous experience, or are you estimating for something you've never done before? What CPTs would be most appropriate for a highly uncertain project?

And what about the number and variety of project stakeholders? Do you have a small, well-aligned stakeholder group or a large and diverse group with varied (and possibly contradictory) expectations of the project? What CPTs best support a diverse project stakeholder community?

The CPTs you choose to bring to the table for a project should be at least as dependent on risk, uncertainty, and stakeholder community as project size. Your response should be flexible but still within a consistent *framework* of CPTs.

Doing the same things, the same way, every time, on every project? That isn't being much more than a project "mechanic." The expert PM, on the other hand, demonstrates a consistent discipline in a considered and *context-appropriate* approach.

And that's what this book represents: a flexible, looser, more stakeholder-aware *framework* of Cs, Ps, and Ts—the competencies, processes, and tools to use as appropriate and to the extent required by the characteristics of the project you're managing.

But don't think for a minute that this looser approach means a lack of rigor and discipline. This book is all about rigor and discipline in areas that *PMBOK® Guide* and PRINCE2 don't cover as well. The CPTs presented here can each be used individually, but they're even stronger when used together, where they complement, support, and interact with each other—and that's where the real strength in the approach lies.

Help Right Here, Right Now, and in Context

Each of the CPTs I'll describe can be used quickly, effectively, and independently of each other, and each should be seen as *adding to* rather than *replacing* the traditional disciplines that project managers and project management organizations have been building up over time.

Although they're *most* powerful when they're used as an integrated set, the CPTs are not prescribed as a comprehensive methodology. Most methodologies are too inflexible to be effective, so this book doesn't propose to represent one. Instead, the book is set up so that you can dip into it at any point, find something you can use right away, and apply it immediately to the situation at hand.

In talking about the CPTs, I'll deliberately focus on project management *context* as much as content, and I'll explain them in the context of real-world situations and real projects I've worked on, and with real examples wherever confidentiality constraints will allow. This approach will, I hope, lead to you to say: "Yeah, I'm in a situation like that, and I can see how that C or P or T will help me in dealing with it."

If I've got it right, this book should enable you to:

- Clearly understand and communicate why a project is undertaken in the first place, and ensure that your measures of success and project stakeholders are aligned accordingly.

- Get control of a project quickly by building a *deliverables-* and performance-based plan that explicitly reflects risk and uncertainty, that demonstrates a clear link to the expectations of the project stakeholder community, and that concentrates on the critically important communications that align the expectations of the stakeholder community right from the beginning and throughout the life of the project.

- Start delivering value early by tracking and communicating the completion of important *deliverables* instead of *activities*. An interesting thing about PMs (and PM tools) and their fascination with activities: No one, especially the executives we report to, really cares much about activities, unless those activities specifically produce the deliverables they *do* care about. In Chapters 13 and 22, we'll talk about measuring and reporting results and *deliverables* as a project progresses.

- Look ahead, to *forecast*, rather than just report on what's happened in the past and on money that's already spent. It seems as if most of our reporting systems are based on telling us what's already occurred, as if that were a satisfactory proxy for forecasting the future. It isn't. Managing a project based on historic reporting seems to me rather like driving a car by looking in the rear-view mirror:

"We're pleased to report that we missed that mailbox one block back, and we're glad to say we didn't hit that fire hydrant, either." We'll talk here instead about forecasting costs, schedules, and the one key element that we tend to report on badly, if at all: project *performance.*

- Finish cleanly and decisively—everyone agrees that we are, indeed, finished—with results objectively reported against measurable, well-communicated, and demonstrable criteria and ensure that project lessons learned are documented and shared across the organization for the benefit of the next project and the next team.

How This Book Is Organized

This book isn't meant to be comprehensive, and you may even call it somewhat selective. What I'm aiming to share here is *additive* information: good stuff that can enrich and add depth to the competent project manager's knowledge.

Throughout this book, we'll take a look at some of our time-honored project management practices that, at times, can actually represent really dumb ideas. We'll talk about the circumstances under which good, traditional PM ideas become dumb ideas and when and where these otherwise good ideas really are best applied. To be clear: I'm not suggesting that these dumb ideas (like steering committees, project kickoff meetings, and red- and yellow- and green-light project status indicators) are inherently bad; most often, they're only really dumb *in the context in which they're used or at the time at which they're applied.* Many otherwise good project management practices become dumb ideas when applied slavishly, sloppily, pedantically ("'cause it's part of the methodology, that's why!"), or at the wrong time.

The first part of the book is about the "guts" of an effective PM, the kind of thinking and acting that underpins everything that follows. Most of this stuff isn't new or radically different, but it certainly isn't common, either.

With the effective "thinking and acting" stuff in place, we'll move to project *planning*, which is unfortunately usually mixed up in the broader definition of project *management*, and that's a mistake. Project planning is a distinct and critically important undertaking that's most often rushed and too often poorly done. Project planning must be seen as a necessary and separate *precursor* to managing a project, and the two shouldn't be confused: project *management* starts after the planning is finished and approved, when management says, "Yes, this makes sense, and the formal baseline [costs, duration and performance], reflective of risk and uncertainty, is now set."

And, by the way, a project should never be "kicked off" before planning is complete because it sends the wrong signal to your stakeholders: "They're kicking off, they must have a solid plan, right?" Without a complete plan, what exactly are you kicking off? If your management is under the impression that your project has started once you begin planning, disabuse them of this incorrect assumption immediately. They need to be made to understand that we don't start to *manage* projects until we have cost, duration, and performance targets to manage against.

Far and away, the biggest part of this book is devoted to project planning, reflecting the work and effort that should be put into it. With planning complete, the project *management* stuff—managing to the plan—is fundamentally a matter of:

- Managing against a well-structured plan (the product of effective project planning)

- A disciplined change-control process, if the planning was done well in the first place

- A steady eye on the measures of success for the projects, those measures of success that arise from the reason(s) the project was chosen in the first place.

So to begin with the guts: Just what kind of fundamental thinking underlies all the Cs, Ps, and Ts covered in this book? What are the "keep it loose, keep it tight" things that we just *feel* in our unconscious, reptilian project manager brains, things that we just *know* in our guts are right, that we can build on and formalize?

The good news is that everything we need to know to be successful is accessible, commonsense, and decidedly nontechnical. It's nothin' you can't handle—let's get started.

Ken Hanley
October 2010

PART 1

THE GUTS OF A GREAT PROJECT MANAGER

By guts, I mean grace under pressure.

—Ernest Hemingway

If PMs listened to their gut instincts a little more ("We missed our dates the last three times out—what makes us think we'll make the date we estimated *this* time?") and paid a little less attention to the tools and rules and software and mechanics, we'd all be better off. And if you're that guy who insists that the first thing your new project management office needs to do is a thorough evaluation of PM software alternatives, you're not helping at all. Tools and rules and software and mechanics are fine in their place, but *only if and after* they're informed by practical, I-know-in-my-guts-that-this-is-true PM thinking—the kind of thinking that the best PMs exhibit regardless of the kind of project they're on, regardless of the tools and rules and software they've got.

And that's what Part 1 of this book is about: the kind of thinking that speaks directly to the good gut instincts of PMs. The next two parts after that will add on the practical how tos: how to apply good project management thinking in planning (the hard part), and then how to manage the project day to day (the easy part, if you do the planning right). But for now, we're talking about the guts-aware thinking that forms the mental framework for effective PMs: the mindset that allows them to connect all the pieces, to see and act on the linkages between risk and uncertainty and the schedule, between the project's stakeholders and its critical deliverables, between its measures of progress and its ultimate project performance, between its priorities and how project changes are handled in light of those priorities. Here's what's in the guts and brains of the best PMs.

CHAPTER 1

A WILLINGNESS TO LEARN FROM THE PAST

It's what you learn after you know it all that counts.

—Harry S. Truman

The best PMs are always thinking about what's in front of them *in the context of what they've learned from the past*. And if that past wasn't always great, they won't blindly, irrationally assume that things will be better this time, especially when there's no evidence to support that optimism. Even if (maybe *especially* if) they hear, "It's different this time, really." Here's what they know: Without a change in thinking and approach, *no, it isn't*.

It's the first question I ask when I'm interviewing PMs: What did you learn from your last project experience? And it's a bad sign if they take a long time answering.

The best PMs are always asking: What have we learned here? And how can we apply what we've learned going forward? More specifically, what have we learned that'll allow us to:

- Repeat the good outcomes, and
- Make sure we don't make the same mistakes again?

It's a key question to ask about any PM or organization that works on projects: has he, she, or it ever made the same project mistakes more than once? If so, they're not learning—not learning about the critical importance of comprehensive project closeout reports (see Chapter 16) or about the importance of planning for and tracking mandatory performance deliverables (see Chapter 9), for example. The best PMs institutionalize learning; they won't compromise on the need to do project closeout reports on *every* project, and you'll see them run reviews at the end of every phase of a project to ensure their team gets better, every step of the way.

Chapter 2

A Need to Know Why

When dealing with people, remember you are not dealing with creatures of logic, but with creatures of emotion, creatures bristling with prejudice and motivated by pride and vanity.

—Dale Carnegie

As far as I can tell, there are two inviolable truths about people and projects:

1. There's a reason behind everything that everyone does on, to, for, with, or against a project. No one does anything without a reason.

2. In a stakeholder's mind, no matter what they are doing on, to, for, with, or against a project, it makes complete sense to them.

The key skill for a PM then, is figuring out: where are these project stakeholders coming from, and most important, why are they acting the way they are? ("Because he's an idiot!" is never the right answer.) The thinking PM asks "Why?" all the time, guided by two principles:

1. He never allows himself to think that someone is doing something "just because he's stupid."

2. He never treats anyone as an "enemy" of the project but, rather, as a potential ally he just hasn't figured out yet.

This approach makes a broad assumption about the intent of the project stakeholder community: It's very rare that a stakeholder is really out to kill a project, even if it feels that way sometimes.

Asking "Why?"—over and over and over again—should take the PM back to root causes. Without an understanding of the root causes of a stakeholder's behavior and their attitude toward a project, the PM probably won't be able to put an effective stakeholder management plan in place.

Getting to Root Causes: The Fishbone Diagram

The fishbone diagram, also known as an Ishikawa diagram or a cause-and-effect diagram, came out of the Japanese quality management push in the 1960s. Although it's more often used to analyze the root cause of product defects, it's also very helpful to PMs in understanding their stakeholders.

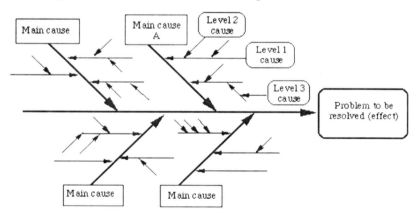

Wikipedia offers this example of root cause thinking[1]:

"My car won't start".

"Why?"

"Because the battery's dead."

"Why?"

"Because the alternator isn't working."

"Why?"

"Because the alternator belt is broken."

"Why?"

"Because the belt was well beyond its service life—it's never been replaced."

"Why?"

"Because I guess I haven't been maintaining my car according to the recommended service schedule."

And *that's* the root cause (although you could keep going to figure out why he isn't maintaining his car, but you get the idea). So how would a root-cause analysis work with a difficult project stakeholder?

Project Business Lead (PBL): "We've invited Bob Miller to the inventory management process redesign sessions a number of times, but he just isn't attending, and that's a problem—Bob's got a lot of influence with the VP of manufacturing."

PM: "Why do we think Bob's not participating?"

PBL: "He says that the way we're tackling process optimization is stupid."

PM: "Stupid how?"

PBL: "He says that we haven't fully considered how things work in his plant."

PM: "Why does he think that?"

PBL: "Because we don't have his warehouse manager on the inventory management redesign team."

PM: "Why not?"

PBL: "Because the COO—our sponsor—chose a warehouse manager from another plant."

PM: "So?"

PBL: "So Bob's warehouse manager had put his name in the hat for that role on the team."

PM: "And... ?"

PBL: "And Bob and his guys are convinced that the next set of promotions will only go to people who are on the project team."

Now we're getting somewhere. Now we're at the root cause, and we have information the PM can act on—something he can take up with the sponsor.

Note

1. Wikipedia, "5 Whys," http://en.wikipedia.org/wiki/5_Whys (accessed August 9, 2010).

CHAPTER 3

A WILLINGNESS TO ASK FOR HELP

He who is afraid of asking is ashamed of learning.

—Danish proverb

The best PMs are always asking for help. It's not because they don't know the answers, and it's not because they don't want to do things for themselves. It's because they understand *the power in asking questions*, and they know that people—sponsors, team members, stakeholders—like to be asked to help and very rarely, if ever, say no when they're asked.

Asking for help says to the people you're asking that you respect their views and that they have a role in the project and a view that's worthy of your consideration. It gives you a chance to voluntarily take yourself off your PM pedestal (if you were ever on one) instead of being knocked off it, and it establishes a collegial relationship with the person you're asking. It's just a good approach in general. Don't ask questions, of course, if you have no intention of listening or responding to what you're hearing; people will see through that kind of disingenuous approach.

PMs should know that they need everyone's help and that if they're not asking, they're missing something. Which is why a common complaint of project managers—"As PM, I have all the

responsibility to get things done, but none of the authority"—
is, I think, somewhat misdirected. That kind of thinking dis-
plays a fundamental misunderstanding of the role of the PM.
The best PMs *don't* have all the responsibility for project outcomes—rather, they share it effectively with people like the
sponsor—nor do they really require all the authority to be successful. The best PMs—and this is probably true of all effective
leaders—rarely exercise their positional power even if they can
do so easily. Instead, they lead by influence and, certainly, by
the will of those they're leading. They ask for help a lot.

Making It *Their* Solution: Leading Others to the Answer You're Looking For

Watch the most successful negotiators (and good PMs are
nothing if not successful negotiators), and you'll see that
they're really good at leading people to solutions that are in
their own best interest while making it look as if the solution was the other person's idea all along. Good negotiators
make it easy for others to come to a conclusion the negotia-
tor's already reached. "I need your help," they'll say. "Here's
what I'm seeing. What are you seeing? What do you think
we should do here?"

If you really do have a solid solution or answer in mind
that makes sense objectively and that you can lay out in
organized fashion, you can reasonably expect the person
you're asking for help will come to the same conclusion. The
difference, of course, is that the *other* person will think that
the conclusion was their idea, and their buy-in will then be
that much stronger. It doesn't really matter whose answer
it is, as long as it's workable; if it comes from one of your

important project stakeholders, all the better. It's a subtle art—just don't be too obvious about what you're doing; people will see through you right away if you are. And remember that this approach *doesn't* work if you've got a really bad idea that you're just trying to jam down someone else's throat. A bad idea, or even a good idea lacking a logical presentation, just won't fly, no matter who owns it.

CHAPTER 4

TAKING DEAD AIM AT OUTRAGEOUS OPTIMISM

We descend into hell one step at a time.

—Charles Baudelaire

In project management, unwarranted optimism is a dangerous thing. Watch out when you hear: "How do you *know* it can't be done that fast?" or "It's different this time" or "You need to be more of an optimist!" These statements imply that the speaker hasn't looked at the historical evidence—or that there is no historical evidence. They're an attempt to appeal to the emotions, with a bit of baseless cheerleading thrown in. Any one of these statements is frustrating; in combination, they're deadly. Fortunately, there are ways to fight back.

Look at What Happened in the Past

We know that some projects, given their schedule, cost, and performance constraints, are headed for the tank right from the beginning, but we just can't *prove* it before they do, largely because we don't have historical success and failure metrics to compare them against. Lacking anything to compare our current projects against, we could end up on projects that are impossible, but not demonstrably so.

To get a realistic sense of what's actually possible on a new project, to avoid falling into the trap of unwarranted optimism, project managers must look at the records from previous projects, which, of course, implies there *are* records to look at. As PMs, we owe it to the entire PM community to produce a complete, disciplined project closeout report for *every* project we work on. We *can't* skip the closeout report, no matter how tight we are on time, and we can't cut corners in completing it. And, as you'll hear many times in this book, a thorough review of previous project closeout reports should be a *mandatory* first deliverable for any new project.

Our friendly neighborhood Project Management Office should be able to dig up prior project charters and the actual results from those prior projects. The baseline plans as reflected in the charters—net of change orders—should line up with the final results... or am I being unrealistic?

If historical information isn't available in our own organizations—and even if it is—we need to pull all the information we can about projects like ours from other organizations, by reaching out to other PMs and other PMOs we know and even some that we don't know—it always helps to build connections in the community.

Once we've gathered historical data from within and without our organization, we need to take notes on the information we find and keep it close at hand as we start planning our new project. The more we read, the more history we'll have, the less susceptible we'll be to those who insist that "it's different this time."

The Gut Check

Does what you're doing *feel* right? If it doesn't, it probably isn't. Listen to your instincts. This advice goes a long way when I'm reviewing failed projects with PMs. I'll ask "When did you first feel the project was in trouble?" "Right at the beginning" is the answer I hear most often.

Allowing for the perfection of hindsight, it's probably true the indicators of troubled projects are evident to the savvy PM *before* their projects even get rolling. If your gut says something's wrong with your planning, it probably is. Keep digging until you figure out exactly *what's* wrong, and don't commit to a date or budget until you do. You might get heat for not moving fast enough, but a lot less heat, I'll bet, than you'll get if that "wrong thing" torpedoes the project later on, after a lot of money's been spent. It's at that point you'll hear: "You're the PM—weren't you supposed to see this coming?"

Remove the Emotion: Use Logic Gates

Emotion makes for better drama, but it's bad for projects and project planning. "You need to be optimistic!" you'll hear, playing to that whole "outrageous optimism" thing that's built into all of us. Optimism is fine in and of itself; it makes the curmudgeons among us tolerable to live with. But *outrageous* optimism is deadly for PMs and their clients.

One of the best ways to take the emotion out of any planning exercise—to reduce the likelihood of making a plan based on hope rather than fact—is to put your project thinking through *logic gates*. Logic gating is a simple but powerful exercise that leads to better, more defensible, less emotional planning. Here's a logic gate exercise that one of my profs led our class through to make a point, and it's stuck with me ever since.

"Here's my proposition A," he said. "I propose to you that all crows are black. Do we all agree that all crows are black?"

Although we were a little concerned that we were being led into a trap—which in fact, we were—we all agreed.

Then he put up a picture of a crow and said, "And here's my proposition B: I propose that the bird in this picture is a crow. Do we all agree that the bird in this picture is a crow?"

We agreed.

And then: "Well, that means that we have *no choice* but to agree with my proposition C: that the bird in this picture is black."

Simple but effective logic jujitsu: Having passed through—and agreed with—the propositions that represented "gates" A and B, we had no choice but to agree with, and step through, the professor's logic gate C, sort of like those one-way drywall screws—once they're in, they don't back out.

So how would this work on a project? Setting: An early-in-the-project team planning meeting, well before the team makes a commitment to a budget or a schedule. The PM says: "OK, do we all agree the project team that management has allowed us to put together for this project is essentially the same one we had last time? The same number of technical people? The same number of subject matter experts dedicating the same amount of their available time? Agreed? Good."

"Now, do we all agree the deliverables on this project are the same size as, or even larger than, those we had last time out? Good."

"And do we all agree it took our team—a team of this size and composition—12 full weeks to get through the analysis phase of the last project? Remember that? Good."

"Then can we all agree the suggestion that the analysis on *this* project should be completed in less than six weeks doesn't make any sense at all, and we should report back to management accordingly?"

Without emotion, with the facts behind us and our sponsor in the room, we should be able to defeat the outrageous optimism in suggesting a six-week analysis phase. We're leading the team and sponsor to a logical and, we hope, more reasonable conclusion about the proposal rather than simply telling them they're wrong. "But it's different this time," someone will surely say. No, it isn't. Insanity is doing things the way we've always done them in the past and expecting a different result this time.

And while we're on the subject of "different this time," don't believe those who say, "It'll be better this time out; we're further up the learning curve." Those who say they've learned to be better or faster without evidence to support such an assertion are like the baker who says, "I know we're losing a dollar on a dozen, but I'm not worried; we'll make it up on volume."

Run It by Others

The PMs who can probably be the most objective (realistic?) about the state of your project are those who aren't directly involved in it. If you've got the opportunity to have someone else look at your project, give 'em everything you've got (preferably before management brings an outsider in and tells you that you *have* to do it). Show 'em everything they're willing to look at; at a minimum, share your first cut baseline schedule and budget, your resources, your constraints and assumptions, and your risk register and risk schedule (see Chapter 19 for a fuller discussion of risk management).

Ask the outside reviewers what they think. If they think "you're dreaming with that schedule," you probably are. Listen to them as carefully as you should be listening to your own gut. And remember that if you're fortunate enough to have someone look at your project without getting paid for it, you've got to be willing to do the same thing for the reviewer on their next project.

Critical Thinking

Evidence of what's happened in the past on similar projects supported by a logic-based assessment of the current project, your gut instincts, and the help of an objective outside assessment should be enough to offset outrageous optimism. Except for the "listen to your gut" part, you can think of this process as "critical thinking for PMs"—it just might save the day, and maybe even your entire project.

Where *don't* we learn enough about critical thinking? In school, I fear. A typical assignment in my class would have asked the students to look at a specific area of project management practice (risk assessment and management, tracking and controls, or stakeholder management, for example) in a specific industry (such as IT, construction, or government capital projects) and then write a paper about it accompanied by a significant in-class presentation. What was I looking for? Papers and presentations that reflected the students' ability to think critically—specifically, to compare and contrast:

- What they'd learned from their research (interviews with practice and industry specialists, for example)
- What they'd been learning in class.

I asked the students to make observations, to *think*, to draw conclusions, and then to make recommendations about improved practices in their own industry based on all of the above.

Fairly straightforward, right?

Unfortunately not. "Compare and contrast... what do you mean by that?" students asked, or "What do you mean by 'draw conclusions and make recommendations'?" and then, almost invariably, "Is this on the test?" Maybe they were just trying to annoy me. If so, it worked. I think I said something like: "I'm fairly certain that both of the words *compare* and *contrast* are in the dictionary," and I'm also fairly certain I restrained myself from asking, "You *do* know how to use a dictionary, don't you?"

So is it possible that we're turning out grade-driven technocrats who can read guidelines, practice suggestions, and bodies of knowledge but can't *think*? And that these people are becoming some of the PMs we're dealing with today? Some of our PMs' behaviors would seem to indicate this is so.

Every PM should be made to take a course or two in logic and philosophy before they graduate from anything. And then maybe we'd get this kind of entirely logical (but maddeningly rare) observation from a PM: "We weren't able to turn out that much clean code in the same period of time on the last project—research shows that no one in the business has been able to turn out that amount of clean code in that period of time—and unless I'm terribly mistaken, we've got the same resources we had last time. So what makes us think that we're going to get a different result this time?" And if they get the response "just make it so," these smarter PMs will find someone else to work for.

CHAPTER 5

SPEAKING UP CLEARLY, EARLY, AND OFTEN

"But he has nothing on at all," said a little child at last.

—Hans Christian Andersen, *The Emperor's New Clothes*

Project problems and challenges shouldn't be hidden. They must be acknowledged and dealt with. The best PMs know we're in a business in which silence is rarely golden and the constant exchange of information is the lifeblood of any successful project. Cognizant of this reality, the very best PMs display several common communication characteristics.

Great PMs Ask Lots of Questions

The best PMs ask questions publicly and communicate the answers widely. They ask the same questions repeatedly to make sure they're getting the same answers from the different people they ask, and they ask the same questions again and again as time passes on a project to ensure continuing alignment. No, they're not deaf or forgetful—they're careful.

Tough questions? Yep. The potentially painful questions that might be uncomfortable to ask up front? You bet. The best PMs know that ignoring or brushing aside issues at the beginning of a project, when we all want to try to get along, means that when the effects of these unresolved issues arise later (and they most certainly will), they'll be that much tougher and much more expensive to deal with. So they take 'em head on and without emotion.

Imagine this scenario in an early project definition meeting:

Marketing VP: "I want to make clear that this project *has* to represent the fastest product launch we've ever had."

CFO: "I want to be clear that I expect this launch to be the most tightly controlled, least expensive project of its kind that we've ever seen."

And the really good PM would be brave enough to say:

> Excuse me, gentlemen… it may just be me, but it seems to me that what you, Mr. Vice President of Marketing, and you, Mr. CFO, are saying is fundamentally misaligned, and that's going to cause problems on this project. I need your help here: Explain to me exactly how you think that this project can be *both* the fastest and the least expensive launch you've ever done? Don't the constraints of one of those requirements fundamentally handicap our ability to meet the other?

Great PMs Don't Assume

How many times have you heard a PM say, "But I put those assumptions in my project plan." The unspoken second half of this sentence is "… and therefore my backside is covered." Here's the news about your project plan: At least half of your project stakeholders probably won't have read it, and even if they did, simply reading about your assumptions doesn't mean that they agree with them.

Assumptions have to be tested up front, publicly, and out loud—hang them on a big banner off the side of the building if you have to. Testing assumptions can put those who don't necessarily agree with those assumptions in a tough spot, and you should expect pushback, but you need to get public alignment and understanding on assumptions (and a lot of other things about the project) before you can start the serious planning.

The best PMs certainly don't assume a questionable piece of information is right just because it came from an executive or someone senior to the project team, and they *never* assume that executives have thoroughly thought through their assumptions before committing them to paper.

Great PMs Repeat Themselves, in a Good Way

The best PMs repeat the important messages, and they confirm an understanding of what was just said. Good presenters do the same thing: Tell 'em what you're going to tell 'em, tell 'em, and then tell 'em what you've just told 'em.

And when these PMs communicate—consistently, regularly, and repeatedly if necessary—they're never in panic mode. Good PMs don't let their projects get to a state where new information could engender panic.

Great PMs Work the Communication Plan

Most project plans I see include some form of communication plan and some type of communications deliverables, but in many cases, these seem to be a formality—something that gets checked off the list when building the charter—rather than a real, integral part of the plan. And integral they should be.

The best PMs share everything they know. If PMs go into a project intending to share information widely and openly, consistent with what's in the communication plan, they establish a pattern in which the extended stakeholder community comes to expect a broad sharing of information. Good PMs understand that it isn't the guy with the most information who's the most effective (and the PM is rarely this guy, anyway) but the person who most actively works the communication channels. It comes down to having open team meetings, meetings to which any project stakeholder is invited to attend if they want to. It comes down to publishing all project status reports on a public website so everyone can see what's going on.

This open approach—really good PMs are never afraid to openly share project information—combined with a willingness and desire to openly ask for help, allows the PM the freedom to call out inconsistencies and issues early in the project process.

Great PMs Focus on Facts and Behavior

The best PMs focus on the *facts* when dealing with project issues ("Here's what we know, as of today..."), and they don't speculate, especially when it comes to the motives of the people around them. And like a marriage counselor, they know that to focus on behavior—"We need to do things differently going forward"—and not personality—"He's always like that; it drives me crazy"—is the best approach.

CHAPTER 6

ALWAYS STARTING WITH THE END IN MIND...

It's not the fall that kills you, it's the sudden stop at the end.

—Douglas Adams

One of the big problems with projects and project managers today is that they start at the *beginning* of their projects. The real pros know to start at the *end* of a project and work backward to the beginning. I know it sounds strange. What I *mean* to say is that the pros first ensure they've got an absolutely clear idea about what the end of their project looks like *before* they start their planning; they know there's no point in planning and scheduling without a clear idea of what they're planning *toward*.

Once they've anchored the end point (as defined by the answer to the first of three key questions in Chapter 9 and made sure their stakeholder community is well aligned on that end point, they'll start planning backward from the end-point deliverables and asking, "What are the *last* things that need to be delivered before we can declare the project at an end? And what about the major deliverables before that? And what about before that?" They'll keep working backward from the end all the way back to the beginning, making note of the dependent deliverables required all the way along the line.

The best PMs know that working backward forces them to consider what must come before and adds discipline to planning. Starting at the beginning? That's for amateurs, and it leads to the *outrageous optimism of forward-based planning.* People will tend to optimistically underestimate the time and effort required to complete a project *if the project end date is set in advance.* How else would you explain all those projects in your organization's portfolio that are scheduled to end on December 31 when, coincidentally, that's also the end of the budget year?

CHAPTER 7

... BUT NEVER STARTING FROM AN END DATE

I love deadlines. I like the whooshing sound they make as they fly by.

—Douglas Adams

Yes, I *know* that your sponsor has an end date in mind already. And yes, I *have* worked on projects for which the end dates just couldn't move. Sometimes they're legislated, sometimes they just "are." For example, the Winter Olympics were scheduled to begin in Vancouver on February 12, 2010, and that date would not be moved under any circumstances. But just because you have a date doesn't mean that the *implications* of that date have been thoroughly thought through. Accepting a date *before* figuring out the implications for project performance (scope and quality) and budget borders on the irresponsible. Sure, there are times when you'll have to back into a project date, but that date should *never* be a part of your first-cut or original plan. Working to a date before anything else has been looked at leads to outrageous optimism.

I saw it in spades a couple of years back with a group of my students at the University of Calgary. It was late April, and the term was almost done. The class? A very bright group all in all: 24 students, all with solid PM backgrounds, half of them working on graduate degrees. I broke them up into three groups of eight, then pulled the first group of eight aside and handed them a fairly detailed statement of work (SOW) for a fictitious project. I also gave them their resource load, detailing how many of each type of person was available to work on their project.

"It's late April," I said to the first group, "and I'd really like to see this project wrapped up by the end of September, if possible. Build me a schedule for class next week, using the resources I've laid out, that shows me how to get the thing done by the end of September." Then I paused. "Keep in mind that I'm a reasonable man, and if you think it *can't* be done by the end of September with the scope as defined in the SOW and the resources I've laid out, let me know. As my old prof used to say, "'If you have to eat crow, eat it when it's young and tender.'" And I sent them on their way.

Then I huddled with the second group of eight. What they *didn't* know was that I was giving them *exactly* the same statement of work and *exactly* the same resource load that I'd given the first group. "It's late April," I said, trying to keep things as similar as possible, "and I'd really like to see this project wrapped up by the end of *November*." Same assignment as before: "If you can, build me a schedule for class next week, using the resources I've laid out." I also gave them the same "I'm a reasonable man" line, and the "eat your crow when it's young and tender" line, and I sent them on their way, too.

Then, over to the third group of eight—you see where I was going with this, don't you—where I gave the same statement of work and the same resource load. But I gave this group the requirement of finishing by the end of *January* the following year and the same "I'm a reasonable man, and let me know if the requirement is unreasonable" speech.

So what do you think I got back from those three teams the next week in class?

The end of January group: "We looked at it really closely," they said, as they handed me their Gantt. "It's going to be tough, but we think we can just make it by the end of January—nine months—with this plan."

And then the end of November group: "It'll be really tight," they said, "but we figure we can just make it with this plan." And they handed in their Gantt.

The end of September group?: "It'll be tough, but we think we can just it squeeze it in."

And that's the outrageous optimism of forward-based planning in its full lack-of-glory. With an arbitrary end date, it's amazing how unrealistically optimistic people can really be.

There's something really powerful about taking a piece of paper with a set (that is, set before anyone has done any planning) end date written on it and then crumpling it up and throwing it over your shoulder with the entire project team—and your sponsor—in the room watching. This isn't meant to be disrespectful of a required end date (and you may want to be a little less dramatic), but it *is* intended to demonstrate a key element in the thinking of the best PMs: The first cut at a project plan should *never* be end-date constrained. Instead, it should be about:

- What needs to be done
- How we'll measure success when we're done
- What resources we have available to get it all done.

Then—and only then, because making decisions about these three elements takes quite a bit of time and thinking—will we try to determine if what we need to do and the *resources we'll have to do it with* are compatible with the end date we've been given. And if it doesn't fit, then we can take a disciplined—not outrageously optimistic—view of *what needs to change* to allow us to make the necessary end date.

- What adjustments can we make to resourcing (and, therefore, budgets) to speed us up?
- Which of our "done" or "won" conditions (see Chapter 9) can we pull off the table or out of the project to help us make the required end date?
- Are there performance compromises (a reduction in scope, quality, or both, perhaps) we can make that'll allow us to hit the required date?

Sure, end dates are important, and they're sometimes established before you know what you've really got to do to make the dates. But they're very often arbitrary and badly misused, and thinking PMs *never* start their planning from them.

Part 2

Planning to Manage

I've said it before: Project *planning* is usually talked about as a part of the broader practice of project *management,* and that causes a problem. Effective project planning really is the *most important* part of managing projects. It's where the project wars are won or lost, and it deserves to be addressed separately, but it usually isn't.

We do ourselves a considerable disservice by referring to what we do as project *management,* suggesting that the *management* piece is the most important part of what we do. It isn't. If project planning is done thoroughly and thoughtfully, the much *less* important piece of the puzzle that follows—managing the project—becomes largely a matter of ongoing stakeholder management and managing against and reporting off of the baseline plan that was established in the beginning. If a complete baseline that addresses duration, cost, and performance (reflecting resources, risks, and uncertainty, of course) is established as the major deliverable of project planning, project management is largely a mechanical exercise of reporting and managing exceptions.

What follows in this part of the book is the really important planning stuff—the hard work associated with building the consensus and cooperation that will allow the (broadly understood, widely accepted) baseline plan to be managed against. This section is the biggest one in the book, and its length very deliberately reflects its importance. It's all about getting to a baseline to manage against, all about *planning to manage*. Once the plan is in place, then the easier stuff begins, the project management stuff, the *managing to the plan* stuff.

We'll start by getting a key element of project success or failure in place: an engaged, active, accountable, and project-educated sponsor.

CHAPTER 8

Sponsor: More of a Verb than a Noun

Here's a sign I'd very much like to see:

Effective Project Sponsors Needed:
Relevant Experience and Education
Definitely Required

The hard truth of it is that many of the people sponsoring our projects aren't qualified to do so. Some aren't experienced enough to be effective sponsors, and even if they are experienced, most haven't been *taught how* to be an *effective* sponsor and what being an effective sponsor means. At their best, many sponsors can be well meaning but, also, less than helpful. At their worst, they can be downright dangerous to you and your project.

So why does this happen? It happens because we have a bad habit of encouraging the "accidental" sponsor. Let me be cynical about this (it won't be the last time) by telling you how project sponsorships are handed out in some organizations: When the senior executives meet and determine, or are dragged into the understanding, that they need to appoint a project sponsor for a major initiative, it's too often a matter of assigning whoever's next: "They say we need a sponsor, and I sponsored that last IT project thingy—it's your turn."

Through some misguided respect for arbitrary authority (and putting someone who doesn't know much about projects at the top of the project heap is about as arbitrary as it gets), and through unthinking deference to seniority, organizations and the project managers in them too often make the mistake of thinking the person or people the executive team has appointed as the sponsors for our projects will be—must be—the "right" sponsors to help make the project a success.

Who Is the Right Who?

Dr. Francis Hartman says the *who* question is probably the most important of the Three Key Questions he asks at the beginning of *any* project (see Chapter 9)[1]:

> Question 1: "For this project, when will we know that we're *done*?" Hartman asks to establish a project end point and an associated set of deliverables that all stakeholders can agree represent the end.

> Question 2: "At the point at which we're done, how will we know that we've *won*?" Here, he's aiming to get agreement among all project stakeholders on the metrics of success for the project, a clear and shared definition of success established well before the project starts.

> Question 3: "Who gets to make the call on questions 1 and 2?" The right sponsor or sponsors gets to declare on behalf of the organization that the project is "done" and the team has "won" by successfully completing the project.

Yes, the most senior person in the organization—everyone says "the president" the first time they're asked—can ultimately make the call on questions 1 and 2, but we're looking for the person further down the organization, the person who is closest to the action, the person that the organization will empower to "make the call" on questions 1 and 2 on its behalf.

Don't be fooled into accepting "figurehead" senior executive project sponsors if they aren't close enough to the project that it won't affect them personally or just because you think they'll have the authority to make decisions. If you do, you'll probably end up with sponsors who have little time for, or interest in, what you're doing.

The great value of experience aside, we need to be able to explain to sponsors that project experience is *different*. No, sponsoring a project is not just like running a division, and it's not just like effectively marketing a product—it's all of this, and *more*, and *different*. And we need to be able to explain that project sponsorship is not an occasional thing but an *active* thing; a verb more than a noun; an important commitment that will demand time, engagement, and most important, *accountability*.

And here's the big kicker sponsors need to be aware of: *Whether a project succeeds or fails, a project sponsor should be accountable for that success or failure, as much or more than anyone on the project team, including the project manager.* And the executive the sponsor works for needs to understand this, too. Accordingly, there are two questions you should ask that'll go a long way toward telling you who the right project sponsor should be:

1. If this project succeeds, will the person or people I'm thinking about as sponsor benefit *directly and visibly* from the project's success?

2. If this project fails, will this person be directly and visibly "hurt" within the organization?

Experience tells me that if the answers to both 1 and 2 aren't a resounding yes, you've got the wrong sponsor.

How Many Sponsors Are Too Many?

One solid, engaged, accountable project sponsor is very good. Two are OK but more difficult to manage. Having more than two sponsors isn't effective at all. What you've got then is a steering committee (a badly executed idea most of the time) trying to act like a sponsor. People sometimes make the mistake of thinking that any exec whose area is affected by the outcome of the project, either directly or peripherally, should have a sponsorship role. No, they shouldn't.

I worked on a financial systems upgrade project in Pennsylvania a few years back where the hosting organization had identified two project sponsors—the CFO and the CIO. So we did our stakeholder analysis carefully and thoroughly (see Chapter 11 for a complete discussion of managing stakeholders' expectations) and came up with a plan and schedule that specifically addressed the expectations of both of these important stakeholders and their organizations.

As expected, the CFO was all about compliance and reporting, and the CIO was all about aligning the new system with his IT road map as well as the systems, standards, and integration that implied. Our plan covered both. But the CFO was all about making an aggressive schedule that he'd already committed to his boss and to the board (the fact that he'd committed to a date *before* a plan was put in place was another issue).

The fact of the matter was that we *couldn't* get the system in on time and still meet all the IT road map requirements and implications of the CIO's expectations. Of course, we could have caved and said we'd do it all on the tight schedule, which would have been a disaster, but I'm pleased to say we stood our ground.

But the problem remained: We had two sponsors with conflicting expectations. At our request (and this had to be handled delicately), the president stepped in. Recognizing that adherence to the IT road map was also an important consideration wherever possible, he made it clear that the date was the most important constraint and asked us to adjust the plan accordingly. He also acknowledged—with the CIO in the room, God bless him—that everything the CIO wanted couldn't be accommodated within the required schedule. The CFO was then designated the single accountable project sponsor, with the CIO as an important member of the project advisory team. The CIO wasn't thrilled with the outcome, of course, but he understood what was required and, more important, that it wasn't the project team who'd told him he couldn't have everything he wanted; it was the president, so he didn't blame us. Sure, we were able to give the CIO much of what he wanted on the project, and he was a supportive stakeholder, but he wasn't the accountable project sponsor, and because of that, we were able to resolve a potential multiple-sponsor conflict.

We assume that if executives have earned enough esteem in their organizations to be assigned such an important role, they must, therefore, also be well qualified to be effective sponsors, right? Wrong. Project sponsors aren't like a good Cabernet; they don't age into greatness, and their seniority often has little to do with their potential effectiveness as sponsors. And too often, their work experience doesn't count for a lot in a project environment. Those who are experts on process—for example, corporate controllers who built their reputation on honing a repeatable process like the month-end close—may be ill-prepared to sponsor a project initiative, where the work is linear and nonrepetitive.

Worse yet, with all their other (i.e., non-project) experience, senior people may fall back on what they know, what's worked for them in the past, regardless of where that experience came from: "I don't think we need to do that formal stakeholder analysis stuff. It's a lot of work, and I don't think we have the time. Let's just get everybody together around a table and work it out—that's always worked well in the past."

Dumb Ideas: Project Kickoff Meetings and Most Sponsors' Roles in Them

Not that a kickoff meeting is a dumb idea in and of itself, but they're a dumb idea when they become purposeless cheerleading sessions: "This is the most important project we've got going in the company today!" says the sponsor (who almost invariably won't have much time for the project team after the kickoff). Never mind that there are three other "most important" projects under way at the same time that are competing for the same resources.

If a project sponsor is prepared and equipped to come out with absolutely clear and usable directions for all those gathered—a very public declaration of the answers to the Three Key Questions, for example—in terms intended to reduce or eliminate uncertainty, that would make for a useful kickoff meeting. But kickoff meetings aren't often working meetings; too often, they are casual and poorly planned meet-and-greet sessions that don't accomplish much more than putting faces to names. Worse yet, a project sponsor might leave such a meeting with the impression that their work is largely done— "I've encouraged the team and set the tone and direction for the project"—when in fact, it's just beginning.

If your kickoff meeting is likely to be nothing more than a social occasion, or if the project sponsor will simply sprinkle a little holy water on the project and then disappear, don't bother having one. Here's a warning sign: Your sponsor says, "I'm really too busy to attend the project planning meetings—go ahead without me." Best advice? Don't. Be brave enough to say, "Your role as project sponsor is critically important to the success of this project, and it doesn't make sense to move ahead with the planning without your direct involvement and input. We'll just have to wait to get started until you have the time." And then you'll want to remind the sponsor that, all things being equal, every day you delay the start of planning (that is, planning *with* the sponsor) is at least one day later the organization should expect the delivery of the project.

Making A More Effective Sponsor

Just knowing all of this doesn't help much, does it? And you're not likely to be well received by a sponsoring executive if you point out that they are probably unqualified for the job. But there are things you can do to help make your project sponsor more effective.

Train and Educate the Sponsor

I'd never propose playing the role of CFO for one of my clients, and certainly not without formal training in finance and accounting first and a lot of experience besides, so it's interesting that some people think a project sponsor might be able to do *that* job without any training at all. Sponsors, just like you and me and anyone else on a project, need to be educated about what it takes to effectively work with a project team. Just as PMs need to be taught to deal with executives, sponsors should be explicitly, deliberately taught to deal with projects, project issues, and project people. They need to learn about change management—the effective trade-off between cost, duration, and performance.

They need to read this book.

The key is to convince them of all of this without causing offense. Senior roles sometimes come with senior egos, and senior egos don't like to be told that they need training. Some advice:

- Unless your sponsors are unusually open minded, don't suggest that they take training with the team. Senior people don't usually like to do that, and certainly not in a situation in which what they don't know might become readily apparent to all the other attendees.

- Suggest that sponsors attend project management/ project sponsorship sessions that are *specifically* run for senior people/sponsors. All of the project management conferences I've attended run special sessions, and even whole tracks, just for the most senior people. When sponsors are in a room with other people whom they see as potential colleagues at the same level, when they're not concerned about showing what they don't know, they tend to be a little more open and a little more receptive to advice on effective sponsorship.

- Ask for their help (this is a really good idea in general, and I'll come back to it a few times). Most people are flattered to be asked for help, sponsors/senior people included. If you tell them how badly you need their support and understanding and how important it is to you and the project that they get up to speed on the PM stuff they're going to have to deal with, how critically important the role of sponsor is to the success of the project, and how much you're looking forward to working with them, you may be able to convince them to spend a little time on up-front sponsor education. And while you're at it, don't call it education; tell 'em that it's an opportunity to "spend time with other senior people like you."

You'd be surprised how amenable people can be to your suggestions when you validate their role and seniority and ask for their help.

Select a Sponsor Deliberately

A project sponsor should never, never, *never* be a figurehead position. As early as possible, make clear the importance and significant contribution required from a project sponsor. Make sure you include a clear and exhaustive description of the role and responsibilities of the project sponsor in every document you produce, as early as possible. The sponsor's duties and how much they're expected to participate must be clear up front. We need to be deliberate and selective about where we need sponsor support—for example, we should specify what we want our sponsor to know about the organizational culture.

If a potential sponsor isn't willing or available to put in the time and energy required per the project charter, do we really want them as a sponsor? I can hear you now: "But I don't get to pick the sponsor, and no one asks what I think about it." You have two choices: Diplomatically but forcefully point out what is needed in an effective sponsor now, before you start the project, or deal with the implications of having an ineffective or unhelpful sponsor later. I know which one I'd choose.

Insist on Sponsor Accountability... Carefully

How brave are you? Brave enough to ask your sponsor, "Is this project on your performance review?" You should be. Yes, it's a tough question to ask, but there are tougher implications later if you don't. Just how engaged do you think a sponsor will be if your (very important) project doesn't have an impact on their performance rating?

While you're working with your team members on their accountability agreements (another very good idea), talk to your sponsor about their accountability agreement, too.

Insist on Sponsor Clarity, Clearly

A project sponsor I worked with last year, who was acutely aware of the political implications of what he was doing, and even more aware of the negative implications of uncertainty and confusion, started us off on the right track by saying:

> "OK, now that I've heard everyone's input, I'm going to make a decision, 'cause that's my job as project sponsor. The decision is option A. The decision is not option B. Does everyone here understand that I've decided on A and not B? Please nod your head to show that you understand.
>
> Let me say this again. Not B, but A. If you were in favor of B, sorry, that's not how it's going to be. Let me be clear about this: No work should be done on B, I don't want to hear about B anymore, the discussion is now closed. All of us are now working on A. Got it? A, not B. Not B, but A."

My kind of project sponsor.

Note

1. Francis T. Hartman, *Don't Park Your Brain Outside: A Practical Guide to Improving Shareholder Value With Smart Management (Newtown Square, PA: The Project Management Justitute, 2000).*

CHAPTER 9

THE INDISPENSABLE THREE KEY QUESTIONS: DONE? WON? AND WHO?

The Three Key Questions (3KQs) are the most powerful of all the CPTs (competencies, processes, tools)—never commit to a project schedule, a budget, or a set of deliverables until the 3KQs are explicitly, objectively, and publicly answered.[1] And I mean explicitly, objectively, and publicly answered such that you and your team and your accountable sponsor would be completely comfortable writing the answers to them on a huge banner and hanging that banner off the side of the building you're working in for everyone to see. In fact, I'd encourage you to do something like that to keep everyone focused on what the project is really all about.

These answers are the anchor points for your plans, and all of your planning from this point forward should directly and visibly connect back to them.

1. **Done:** What set of deliverables will tell the entire stakeholder community that the project is *finished*?

2. **Won:** What set of deliverables, reflecting objective measurements of success, will tell the entire stakeholder community that the project has been *successfully* delivered?

3. **Who:** Who is *publicly and explicitly accountable*, on behalf of the organization hosting the project, for answering questions 1 and 2?

Although the PM framework I'm suggesting is flexible in the sense that you can choose which parts you use and to what extent you use them depending on the characteristics of your project, *the Three Key Questions aren't.* They're so foundational, so centering, so fundamental that they should be used in the planning for *any* project of *any* kind or *any* size.

Think about how effective the answers to these questions can be in helping you keep your project on track. Combined, they create that clear mission statement every PM book ever written says your project needs:

> "What's this project about, you ask? Let me tell you: We'll be a *roaring success* if we deliver these X things; we'll be *done and finished* when we deliver these Y things; and Sponsor Z will be the one *accountable,* on behalf of the organization, for declaring that we're finished and that we've been successful. And thanks for asking."

I'd argue that if you can't land on a set of clear answers to the 3KQs every major stakeholder can agree to, you've got, by definition, an unmanageable project. Imagine starting a project without having a clear and shared understanding of when it will end *in advance.* Without understanding its measures of success *before* it gets started? Without clear sponsor accountability? Unfortunately, this happens all the time.

The 3KQs can help put an end to that. By their nature, they provide:

- An end point to plan toward
- The objective measures of success
- A clear understanding of accountabilities.

Let's talk about the 3KQs that were used on a project to replace an aging, patchworked customer call-handling system. The client was dissatisfied with its unintegrated systems and was unhappy about how long it took its customer support staff to access the information they needed to answer questions for their customers when those customers phoned in to the call center. Customer support staff had to go back and forth from screen to screen to find related customer information and had to rekey customer account numbers as they moved from screen to screen around the system.

On top of these problems, the Vice President of Customer Care said, "It's costing us way too much to operate the system we have now, and we've got too many people in our call center compared to our competitors—way above industry average for the number of calls we deal with in a month. And because we're slow in getting the information our customers want when they call, they aren't nearly as happy with us as we'd like them to be."

Let's turn those broad requirements into a specific set of deliverables for the project—some of them "wons" and some of them "dones."

Question 1: Done?

So what would "done" look like for this project? The manager of development for the client's IT shop thought the project would be done, from his perspective, when the new software supporting the call center had been successfully tested and moved into production.

The manager of the help desk went further. "Look, we can't declare this thing 'done' just because the system's up and running before the guys on my help desk have got all the quirks and nuances of the new system figured out, and that usually takes weeks after a system goes into production. We can't just declare victory and walk away while we're still figuring this stuff out."

The team's business subject matter expert (SME), who represented the frontline customer support representatives, went even further: "It's more than just getting the help desk up to speed. Maybe we should let the system stabilize for at least a couple of months—let it settle in a bit for the people using it—before we call a wrap to the project."

Everyone seemed to agree, and as the PM, I sure liked the idea of everyone landing on a common end point, knowing that all sorts of confusion and misalignment would result if we couldn't agree on a single point. So, we set the end of a 60-day settling-in period, with a full report on the operational and support status of the system as the deliverable, as the "done" point for the project. I wrote a description of the deliverable down on a Post-it® note, in big black letters that could be seen from across the room, and labelled it with a "D" (see Figure 9.1).

That Post-it® note represented an anchor deliverable for the project—a clear definition of what constituted "done." It was soon to be joined by dozens of more deliverables, all part of the project's drop dead date schedule (see Chapter 12). Agreeing on the end point for the project kept us from letting a "sort of" ending bleed messily into operations (a common problem) because we were able to definitively establish when the project ended and when operational support began.

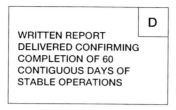

Figure 9.1 A "Done" Deliverable

When We Don't Align on "Done"

A project I was asked to take a look at few years back was significantly misaligned about its end date. The team was made up of competent professionals—so far, so good—all hard drivers who had little patience with planning and just wanted to get the thing done. The "thing" in question was a shallow natural gas drilling project in eastern Alberta involving the drilling of more than 100 wells in quick succession and a budget in the tens of millions.

I got to ask the team what I thought were some fundamental questions, at the request of their boss, the VP of Exploration, who was looking for a tighter budget estimate and a schedule that showed all the wells drilled, completed, and tied-in by break-up. (Break-up is the time in the spring during which the frozen ground thaws out, and the roads get so wet and muddy that heavy equipment like drilling rigs can't be moved on them, and road bans for heavy vehicles are put in place to protect the roads.)

"Bear with me, guys," I said. "I know you've got the rigs rolling, and you're anxious to start drilling, but just answer a question for me: When are you done with this project?" I got a look around the table that suggested they'd rather do almost anything other than answer stupid questions from a stupid consultant.

The PM, a senior geologist, spoke first: "It's pretty straightforward; this is a development play, stepping out from wells we're already producing from. We're done when we've drilled the new wells, proved the gas volume, and booked the reserves."

The field engineer hesitated. "Yeah, I guess so, but we can't really say 'done' 'til we've got the surface facilities in place to handle that gas, right?"

"Not really," said the engineer responsible for field pipelines. "The gas doesn't do us any good until we can move it to a plant, does it? I always thought that 'done' would be when we'd connected those wells to the plant with new pipe."

A murmur went around the table, and then the facilities engineer spoke up: "When you think about it, we're really not 'done' until the two gas plants in the area get their treatment and processing upgrades—I've always said they can't handle the volume we're predicting from these new wells the way they are now."

Before I could say anything the manager of operations for one of the two gas plants in question said, "It's not just a matter of upgrading the facilities—it's a matter of making sure we can stabilize production volumes over a couple of months before we call it 'done.' My operations guys fought with a plant upgrade for three months last winter after engineering said it was supposed to be finished."

I thought my point had been made, but they weren't done. The marketing guy, who usually didn't say much in these team meetings, spoke up: "Look, this project really is about getting gas to our customers, isn't it? If we can't move it to where they need it, the extra production doesn't mean anything. We've committed 20 mcf [millions of cubic feet] a day of this new production to a big client in Sarnia, Ontario, under a two-year contract, and we really aren't done, are we, until we've met those delivery obligations?"

And then the environmental advisor chimed in: "If we're really talking about 'done,' I don't think we're *really* done until we've produced all the gas we can from those facilities, shut 'em down, and reclaimed the property they sit on—all the gas out, and cattle grazing where the gas plants used to be—now *that's* done."

I didn't have to say anything, but I couldn't resist: "Let me get this straight: You're all working on the same project, and your boss needs a tighter budget and schedule for the project, and you've got an end date that looks like something between six months and fifteen years?

Stupid time-wasting consultant aside, they agreed that they probably should settle on a single project-end deliverable and schedule and budget accordingly.

Question 2: Won?

The question to ask here: At the point at which we're done with this project, how will we know that we've "won"? That is, which deliverables will visibly, objectively show the world that we've been successful? Every answer to this question should be represented in your plan by at least one deliverable and probably more.

Let's say that the following three measures would indicate the customer call-center support system project was successful:

1. Reduce average call-handling time from four minutes per call to less than two minutes per call

2. Reduce call-handling staff count by 30 percent

3. Increase customer satisfaction ratings such that 85 percent or more of our clients are saying we're doing a great job—25 percent above the 60 percent who think we're doing a great job now.

For this project, the "won" measures arose from adding some discipline and objective measures to the requirements the client had been talking about. After some work with the sponsor and team, we came up with these three "won" deliverables:

1. We've reduced the average call-handling time for calls to our call center from more than four minutes today to less than two minutes, as indicated by the new system's call logs.

2. We've reduced our call-handling staff by 30 percent (probably a reasonable "won" measurement given the first deliverable) and moved those staff to other roles in the organization.

3. We've increased customer satisfaction such that 85 percent of our customers would rate our help desk a 4 or 5 out of 5 (on a scale in which 1 is terrible and 5 is excellent), up from 60 percent of customers giving the help desk the same ratings, based on a survey of customers who called the customer call center after the new system was operational.

These measures need to be clear and unambiguous. No, neither "We'll all like it a lot" nor "It has to be better than

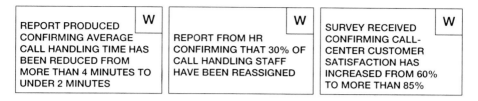

Figure 9.2 A "Won" Deliverable

the one we have" are adequate measures of success, and anything subject to interpretation makes a bad "won" deliverable. Just as we did for the "done" deliverable (which was a report on the new system's operational and support status), I wrote each of the "won" deliverables on Post-it® notes in big black letters and marked each with a "W" so they'd stand out (see Figure 9.2). These were added to the drop dead date schedule, too.

"Done" and "Won" Deliverables Sometimes Get Confused

Teams sometimes mix up "dones" and "wons," especially the first few times they use the 3KQs. Example: My daughters and I like to surf on the west coast of Vancouver Island, and the "project" to get there from Calgary in the Jeep has its own set of "dones" and "wons."

"Done" deliverables tell us that we're finished, but they don't say anything about how well we did in getting *to* done. In our case, there were two done deliverables:

1. The tent was pitched just behind the beach

2. The surfboards were waxed and ready to go

Even with these deliverables in hand, the "project" necessary to get to them could have been a disaster, so our trip also had "won" deliverables. The measures of success could be articulated in three very specific deliverables:

1. The driving trip took under two days.

2. We burned less than five tanks of gas.

3. My two daughters, sitting in the back seat, didn't kill each other en route.

"Done" deliverables are objective measures of being finished; "won" deliverables are measures of how well the thing was finished.

Question 3: Who Gets to Make the Call on Questions 1 and 2?

This is the question that points us right to our sponsor. If the answer to "who" isn't your project sponsor (or two sponsors, if you must)—if it doesn't clearly identify the person responsible and accountable for answering questions 1 and 2 on behalf of your organization—then just *who* is the who? If it isn't clear who's charged with answering questions 1 and 2, stop now and figure it out. If accountability isn't clear, you've got a larger problem that'll come back and bite you later.

The "who" person should be the visible, public sponsor. You'll want to have them sign off on the answers to questions 1 and 2—maybe on the big banner you'll be hanging outside the building. They should be willing to have these answers widely publicized and directly associated with their name.

Make the "Won" and "Done" Deliverables Stand Out in Your Project Plan

As part of the broader agenda of focusing more on project deliverables (which everyone cares about) and less on project activities (which no one except the project mechanics really cares about), deliverables that connect directly to the "done" and "won" answers should stand out in your plan.

Remember that the "done" and "won" deliverables in the call-center project stood out from all the other deliverables because we wrote a big "D" on the "done" deliverables and a big "W" on the "wons." Calling out the "dones" and "wons" in your schedule—the schedule that you're going to be using when you discuss the project with your stakeholder community—makes a deliberate and explicit connection between the schedule you're building and the foundation answers about the substance of your project, as articulated in the 3KQs.

I'll go further and say if you can't readily see the "done" and "won" deliverables in the schedule you're presenting, your schedule is too far removed from the key measures of success—in other words, it's too abstract—to be relevant to the great majority of your project community. And that, by the way, is one of the reasons senior management and the non–project-specialist stakeholder community don't really care about, or pay much attention to, any Gantts or PERTs you put in front of them. These documents may mean something to we PMs, but not so much to them. They're full of activities and predecessors and start-finish relationships—the kind of things non-PM people think that we PM people should be worrying about—but they don't speak to what the stakeholders care about. They care about measures of success, major deliverables, and key milestone dates, and if these things don't stand out in your schedule, they're not likely to pay much attention. On the other hand, if your sponsor agrees to the "done" and "won" deliverables, they are sure as heck going to want to see that those deliverables are right there in your project schedule, too.

The Mechanics of Answering the Three Key Questions

You shouldn't tackle the Three Key Questions without the active and enthusiastic involvement of your sponsor and as many of the other project stakeholders as are available. Although it may make sense to put a rough draft of the answers to the 3KQs together for review with the sponsor, it's critical that the sponsor take ownership and accountability for the answers. I've had to have a few conversations like this at the beginning of a project:

"Greg, we want to start up the planning on that project you guys discussed at the executive meeting last week, and we need to know when we can have a solid half-day of your time to answer some key questions about it, and then another couple of days in the next two weeks after that to confirm our plans and start to lay out a schedule."

"So why do you need me?"

"Because you're the sponsor and, as such, you'll be accountable for the answers to those questions."

"I'm really busy what with budget coming up and all... can't you guys get going without me?"

"No, we can't. This is how projects get in trouble around here—the project team trying to guess what it is you're looking for in the end and usually getting it wrong."

"Look, I've got more than a full-time job right now managing what's already in my lap, and you've got a good team there. Why don't you get started, and I'll jump in when I need to?"

"When you *need* to? I thought you guys said that this project was the number-one priority for the company for this year?"

"Yeah, but you know how many number-one priority projects we have around here…"

"And that's part of your problem."

"Pardon me?"

"Never mind. If this project really is as important to the success of the company as you say it is, we'll need your time and attention in the planning."

"You're not going to make me look at Gantt charts, are you?"

"No. We need you, on behalf of the company—you are the accountable sponsor, after all—to confirm the project's measures of success, to understand and help us manage the expectations of all the project stakeholders, and to make sure that everyone is aligned on things like when the project stops being a project and moves into an operational mode. And about those stakeholder expectations—I'm going to need your help in resolving conflicts between them."

"Isn't that your job as the project manager?"

"No, it isn't. I can identify potential expectation conflicts when we see them, but you're the guy who represents the will of the business. I'll bring them to you for resolution, and I'll tell you the implications for budget and schedule and project performance for any decisions that you make, but those decisions are yours to make as the key representative of your organization—that's what being a sponsor is all about."

"But we don't usually get all that involved in those kinds of things."

"Yeah, and that's a problem, too. You guys have been figurehead sponsors on all the projects you've had trouble with to date, and that's got to stop."

"All right, all right, I'll be there, but I probably can't free up that much time until the beginning of next month."

"If that's the case, we'll suspend any project activities until you're available and disband the team until you're available to work with us. We need you to participate in planning our starting point, and we can't start without you. And by the way, for every day we delay now, we'll have to tack a least a day onto the end date."

"But you know as well as I do that this thing is time sensitive—we can't afford to go later on the end date. Can't you get started on other stuff?"

"What other stuff? Everything hinges on some basic understandings. Without a clear understanding of the measures of success or what the end point of the project looks like, we can't do anything."

"Fine," Greg said, not smiling. "I'll get my assistant to clear Monday afternoon."

"And two more half days the week after that. And also have her schedule a standing meeting between you and me for an hour every week—I get the feeling there's going to be a whole bunch of stuff we're going to need your decisions on. I'll ask our subject matter experts to take a first crack at defining the objective measures of success, but you'll have to be comfortable with approving, owning, and communicating them."

"Anything else you need?"

"Yeah, everyone on the team wants to know if this project is on your performance review, and if not, why not?"

Watch for "Wons" That Occur After the Last "Done"

A common error project teams make is declaring an end to the project before the "won" deliverables can be delivered—before they are measurable. This happens all the time. There's an understandable conflict between wanting to finish a project up in a reasonable time—and scheduling accordingly—and wanting the measures of success for the project to be business oriented, measurable, and durable.

The key to timing "won" deliverables correctly is ensuring that all of them are scheduled to occur at the same time as or before the last "done" deliverable. You should be able to measure and verify all of the deliverables you've said will tell you that you've won before you put down your tools and declare the project finished.

This problem came up on our call-center support system project. We'd said that "done" for the project would be represented by the completion of the go-live operational and support status report. Let's check our report against the "won" deliverables:

- *A reduction in average call-handling time from four minutes per call to less than two minutes per call.* Would we get enough call volume through the system in the three months following go-live to prove that we'd been able to drive a sustained reduction in average call time? Our sponsor said yes: "With the good pre–go-live training system for the call staff we've planned and 12,000 support calls per month—36,000 by the time we get to 'done'—we should be able to get that call-handling time down to the two-minute target and keep it there." Good.

- *A reduction in the call-center head count by 30 percent.* We had to check with our HR rep on the team regarding this one. Was it possible to have the three customer support reps (30 percent of the customer-support-center staff of ten) we'd planned to move out of the customer-support call center retrained and working in their new areas of the company within three months of go-live? We knew the real trigger here was the point at which the reps' salaries would be transferred to a different cost center and the customer-service-center salary costs reduced accordingly. Our HR rep confirmed that yes, the three employees would be in their new roles and their salary costs would be picked up by their new work unit within 90 days of go-live. So far, so good.

• *Increase customer satisfaction (as indicated by 4/5 or 5/5 ratings) to more than 85 percent.* This one complicated things. When we discussed the deliverable that would give us the customer-satisfaction measures we were looking for, the Vice-President of Customer Care pointed out a problem: "I don't know how you're going to get those customer-sat scores in before you end the project. We don't survey anything new 'til we've been using it with customers for at least six months." And therein lay the problem. We were proposing to end the project three months after go-live, but we were also proposing to declare victory, that we had "won," on the basis of improved customer satisfaction numbers—numbers that wouldn't be available to us until at least six months after go-live (see Figure 9.3).

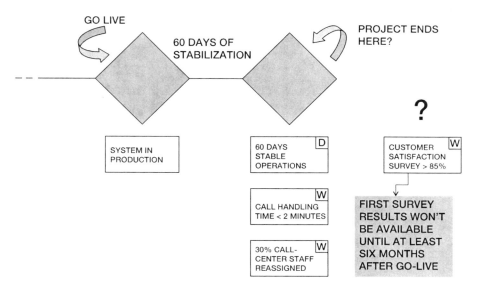

Figure 9.3 A "Won" Deliverable That Occurs After the Project

And that's where we had to be sure we lined up the "dones" and the "wons" on the project; we had to make adjustments in our planning to ensure that the last (latest-occurring) "won" deliverable was scheduled at the same time as or before the last "done" deliverable.

The project team had two choices:

1. Drop the customer-satisfaction-increase deliverable as a measure of success for the project because we couldn't achieve it by the time we'd be "done" three months after go-live (see Figure 9.4)

2. Extend the project to incorporate the measure of customer satisfaction, and extend its end date ("done") to at least six months after go-live, when the customer survey could be completed (see Figure 9.5).

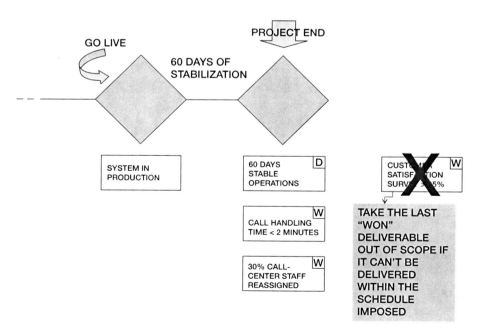

Figure 9.4 Delete a "Won" Deliverable

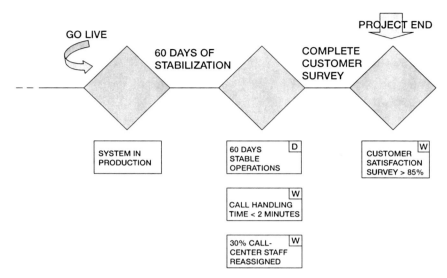

Figure 9.5 Extend the Project End Date

The ensuing discussion was animated but absolutely necessary. Sure, it would cost more to keep the project running for six months after go-live (but not a whole bunch more because most of the team members could return to their prior positions during the six-month stabilization period), but then the team could declare an end to the project with all measures of success—all "won" deliverables—completed and, most important, be seen as a success in the eyes of the broader stakeholder community. And that's what we ended up doing.

Note

1. Francis T. Hartman, *Don't Park Your Brain Outside: A Practical Guide to Improving Shareholder Value With Smart Management* (Newtown Square, PA: The Project Management Institute, 2000).

CHAPTER 10

USING THE PROJECT PRIORITY TRIANGLE EFFECTIVELY

PMs talk about the triple constraints of project management and their visual representation, the project priority triangle, all the time. Problem is, we talk about these generically, without specifically applying them to how we manage our projects and our relationships with our sponsors. "It's not possible to incorporate changes in a project," we'll say, "without having an impact on the project's cost, its duration, or its performance." We know that this is true, but we don't integrate it into our projects in the most effective way. Specifically:

- We tend to acknowledge it amongst ourselves, but it's much more powerful to discuss it with our sponsors and clients in the active context of the project we're working on.

- When we do talk with our clients about the need to make trade-offs in light of changes to our projects, we tend to use it as a bat to smack them with ("If you want to make that addition to scope without moving the end date or dropping something else, you know it's going to cost more!") rather than as the communication and problem-solving vehicle it should be.

Used properly, the project priority triangle allows PMs to engage their sponsor early and often, to ensure that project priorities are discussed in advance, and that a clear and explicit direction for accommodating changes is documented and communicated to the project team and to the broader project stakeholder community.

Reading the Project Priority Triangle

The three corners of the project priority triangle are:

- Cost
- Duration
- Performance (see Figure 10.1).

This triangle will look different than the one you're used to seeing for one very important reason: the third corner. You're used to seeing *cost* (sometimes *budget*) and *duration* (sometimes *schedule*) as the first two corners. In this triangle, *performance* takes the place of what you usually see in the third corner: *scope*. That's because scope isn't, in and of itself, adequate to describe the third constraint. In addition to cost and duration, there are *two* elements that can flex in response to a change:

1. ***Scope, or how much you will or won't do.*** You can accommodate a change without affecting cost or duration

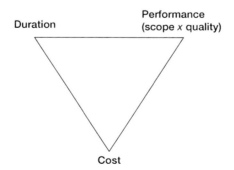

Figure 10.1 A Basic Project Priority Triangle

by reducing the *amount* of work that you do. Leaving out certain functionality in an application in agreement with your sponsor would, for example, reflect a decrease in scope in response to a change.

2. *Quality, or how well you do it.* You can accommodate a change without affecting cost or duration by reducing the *quality* of one or more of your deliverables. Compromising on your "won" deliverable by agreeing with your sponsor that the average call-handling time for the customer call center should be reduced to two-and-a-half minutes, rather than the original two-minute target, would be a decrease in quality, for example.

Combining scope and quality and representing them collectively as *performance* on the third corner of the triangle reflects the fact that any decrease in scope, quality, or both will, in fact, have a negative impact on project performance—that is, its ability to deliver what was originally committed.

Cost

Placing an X in this corner indicates that staying at or under the project budget is the most important consideration when considering a change. By putting an X in the cost corner, the sponsor is telling the project team that it should look to other solutions if possible—such as pushing out the end date or reducing project performance—to accommodate changes as they arise, instead of increasing the project budget.

Duration

The sponsor places an X in this corner to tell the team that keeping to the original end date—avoiding a late project—is the most important consideration. When faced with changes, the project team should consider spending more money or compromising performance instead of doing anything that might delay the project completion date.

Performance

An X in this corner indicates that keeping to the budget and schedule are less important than maintaining project performance. The sponsor would rather see the team push out the project end date or increase the budget than compromise the planned performance of the project as reflected in the measurable "won" deliverables.

Using No-Go Zones

When you ask your sponsors, "What's the most important thing in this project: making the due date, keeping to the budget, or delivering on everything we said we would with the quality we'd planned?" their answer will likely be, "They're all important." Further, if you were to ask your sponsors to place an X on the project priority triangle to reflect the relative importance of these constraints, they'd likely put it right in the middle, which doesn't tell you anything helpful at all (see Figure 10.2).

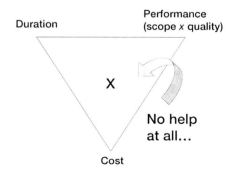

Figure 10.2 An Unhelpful Project Priority Triangle

And that's probably because you're asking the wrong question. Try this one on for size with your sponsor:

"We all understand that project duration and budget and performance are important on this project, and we're working hard to ensure we run to the original plan. What we're asking is this: If something *changes* that we have to accommodate in the project, which one of the three is the *most* important? If something changes in the project environment—maybe a new piece of required functionality that wasn't in the original plan—which of our 'change tools'—cost, duration, or performance—do you want us to use *first* to accommodate that change?

"Would you prefer us to accommodate those changes by

- Increasing the budget
- Extending the schedule
- Degrading performance? We could do that by cutting back on other functionality [cutting the scope] to make room for the change, or we could cut back on quality—how well we might deliver some functionality. We may, for example, only be able to cut average call-handling time to two minutes and 30 seconds, instead of the two minutes we originally anticipated.

"We're not asking for an excuse to run late or go over budget or under-deliver. What we are looking for is your guidance *in advance* so that if a change does come up, we'll know which change options to look at first, and we'll know how to tackle it in line with your expectations.

"If you tell us that budget is the number-one priority, we'll look at change options that might affect schedule and performance. On the other hand, if you tell us the schedule [duration] is number one, then we'll look at solutions that might increase the budget or affect performance. If you tell us that performance is number one, we'll look at solutions that might mean pushing out the end date or spending more money than originally planned."

To determine which constraint *really* is the most important and to avoid the "they're all important" determination that the team doesn't know how to respond to, you may want to add to the triangle what my prof Francis Hartman called "no-go zones" in class (see Figure 10.3). When no-go zones are added to the triangle, there are only six places for the X to go—the numbered zones shown in Figure 10.4, each of which gives explicit direction to the project team about how the sponsor would like changes handled and clarifies the relative importance of cost, duration, and performance in light of potential project changes. The sponsor can mark any of six places to indicate the project constraint that the team shouldn't "touch" because the sponsor considers it the top priority.

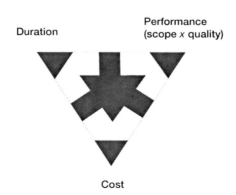

Figure 10.3 Project Priority Triangle with No-Go Zones

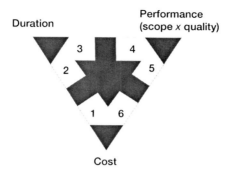

Figure 10.4 Project Priority Triangle with Numbered No-Go Zones

An X in location 1, for example, indicates that the sponsor considers the project budget the first priority, and because the next-closest corner is the duration corner, they're also telling you that schedule is the next most important constraint. The message is: "If we have to accommodate a change, my preference would be that you look at reducing project performance [reducing scope or quality or both] first. The project budget is the most important consideration of the three, so don't consider changes that will increase the budget. The schedule is also important (but not as important as budget), so any schedule adjustments should only be considered after you look at reductions in project performance."

An X in location 4, nearest the performance corner, communicates to the team that project performance is the top priority; when changes arise, the sponsor prefers that they be addressed in ways that do not compromise the project's scope or quality. Because the X is next closest to the duration corner, they're also saying that the schedule is important, too—less important than performance, but more so than the budget. In this case, the PM could accommodate the change by getting additional project funds, so that project performance and, if possible, the schedule, wouldn't be negatively affected.

Likewise, an X in:

- **Location 2** indicates the sponsor has directed that project schedule (duration) is most important, followed by the budget (cost)

- **Location 3** indicates the sponsor has directed that project schedule (duration) is most important, followed by performance

- **Location 5** indicates the sponsor has directed that project performance (scope × quality) is most important, followed by the budget (cost)

- **Location 6** indicates the sponsor has directed that project budget (cost) is most important, followed by performance.

Because project change management can be an inexact science—for example, it may not be possible to extend the end date of the project without also increasing costs, especially if you have consultants or contractors on your project team—it's important to note that the priority triangle should be used more as a guide than a dictate. The sponsor should reasonably expect the PM to consider options for accommodating changes as they arise in light of the broad priorities communicated through the priority triangle, but they must understand that there may be exceptions that will need to be discussed. Regardless, changes should be handled in a way that's consistent with the direction indicated by the triangle, or your triangle's wrong.

Managing With the Triangle

Things change during the life of a project, not least because the environment in which the project is being executed changes, and effective PMs adjust accordingly. They know that just because the priority triangle at the beginning of the project showed that the project schedule was the number-one driver, that doesn't necessarily mean it'll stay that way throughout the whole project. That's why the priority triangle—and where the X sits at the start of each reporting period—should appear on every project status report and be reviewed regularly with the sponsor.

Consider a project for an oil and gas producer. The company's expectation of how its project teams should best handle changes as they arise could be heavily influenced by commodity price swings. When oil prices are rising quickly, as they did in early 2008, the producer might make the project schedule priority number one: "Let's get that valuable production and cash flow on line as quickly as possible," the sponsor might say, "even if it does cost us a little bit more to make an early date." If oil prices fall quickly, however, as they did later the same year, the same sponsor might reasonably say, "With these prices, we've got to manage our cash carefully—if that means slowing the project down to preserve capital this year, that's what we'll do." Two different priorities and two different expectations of how the project team will behave in light of changes on the same project, within the same year. The PM should expect to have to adjust the team's approach in light of these changes, but they should also expect the sponsor to communicate these changed expectations via the priority triangle.

If the priority triangle appears on the status report every week, it's a visible reminder to the PM and the sponsor to recheck project drivers on a regular basis. If priorities change—if budget becomes more important than schedule, for example—the change should be reflected on the status report itself.

When the priority triangle changes—from a priority on date rather than on performance, for example—with specific instructions from the sponsor, you'll probably want to highlight that change on your status report by putting a big red circle around it so that everyone sees the change and understands how the project might be managed differently going forward.

CHAPTER 11

MANAGING STAKEHOLDERS' EXPECTATIONS DELIBERATELY, EXPLICITLY, AND EFFECTIVELY

A project stakeholder is anyone who can have an impact on, or be impacted by, the project. That's a pretty broad definition, and deliberately so. Experienced PMs know that there's usually a broad community out there with an interest in the project they're working on. This includes the project sponsor and the organization hosting the project, obviously, but it also encompasses all of the partners and project team members (very much including you as the PM) and a whole bunch of other people and groups you normally wouldn't think about. After getting alignment on the answers to the Three Key Questions, it makes sense to turn your attention to the project stakeholder community next.

- *Who* are your stakeholders?
- *What are they expecting* from the project?

- What does the project team have to *deliver* to meet those expectations?

And while we're at it, are there any stakeholder expectations that the project *can't* or *won't* meet? Do any of those stakeholder expectations *conflict* with the expectations of any other project stakeholder?

Aligning the Project Team

Forget about trying to get the broader stakeholder community aligned if you can't get your own project team members (key stakeholders themselves) all rowing in the same direction. Alignment among team members is determined, declared, and then demonstrated through daily interactions. Coming to a shared and public agreement on how the project team is going to work together is a good start.

Depending on the personality of the organization and your team (some people love this kind of thing, but some find it as objectionable as those awful inspirational posters that hang in some offices), this team agreement can be discussed, distributed to the team, or printed on a big piece of paper hung on the wall in your project war room.

On a recent, multinational project team, we had a couple of real teamwork enthusiasts who suggested that team members contribute their national flags to the otherwise dull decor of the project room. We had big flags up from Canada, France, India, China, and South Africa; I contributed my usual skull and crossbones.

The teamwork enthusiasts suggested that we put our team intent, our collective will, whatever you want to call it, down on paper (a big piece of paper) that everyone would sign on the same day that our project sponsor signed the project charter. Here are the agreements we made and listed on that big piece of paper, which hung on the wall in our war room throughout the project. (And yes, we did refer to the poster a couple of times when things got a little tense.)

- *We agree that if one group or member of the team fails on this project, we all fail.* It is not possible for any person or any group to be successful on this project if any other person or other group fails; we will all receive the lowest mark that the lowest performing member or group receives. It is up to us as a team to ensure that we are all successful. If the project goes badly, none of us will look good, even if the problem was someone else's fault. As the saying goes, "We can hang together, or we can hang separately."

- *We agree to come to decisions through consultation, and we'll consult with each other broadly.* In areas in which we don't explicitly agree, we will respectfully and publicly escalate disagreements. We all agree to respect and act in alignment with decisions that come about as the result of escalation, even if we don't personally agree with the decision.

- *We agree that we'll make assumptions about absolutely nothing.* We will not make assumptions about what other people understand or what they know. We will assume that unless we have clear and specific understandings in writing, these understandings do not exist. Assume that if a point is not clear enough for someone like Ken to understand (and that has to be pretty clear and straightforward), our communications aren't clear enough.

- *We agree to put our communications and understandings in writing and always make them accessible to everyone else on the team.* We'll set up a common, widely accessible location for all project information, with the assumption that any of us should be able to find out anything we want or need to know about the project at any time.

- *We agree to overcommunicate.* We agree that as far as is practical, we will put everyone else on the team on our email Cc lists when we're communicating practically anything about the project. If people on our team see a message that is irrelevant to them, they can decide to delete those messages, but let's give each person on the team the opportunity to make that decision for themselves. Not communicating with other team members because we "don't think they need to know" or "they should already know this" is unacceptable. Under no circumstances whatsoever is it acceptable for any of us to say or think "I didn't know" about something associated with the project.

- *We agree to ask each other for help.* By asking for help, we agree that we are dependent on the skills and knowledge of our fellow team members to be successful, we demonstrate respect for other members of our team, and we enhance our ability to create solutions that take best advantage of the skills we have across the team. We agree that asking for help does not imply a lack of competence; it is an important communication skill.

Making Stakeholder Expectations Drive the Project Plan

It comes down to this: Stakeholder perspectives must be the primary driver of your project plan. Further, if project stakeholder expectations are not *explicitly* visible in your project schedule, you've got a problem. There must be a deliberate and visible linkage between the expectations of the stakeholder community and the deliverables in the project plan; specifically, deliverables in the schedule should be coded to one or more stakeholders and the expectations they have of the project. (If there's a deliverable in your schedule that no stakeholder cares about, why is it in your schedule in the first place?) The will of the stakeholder community must be explicit in the project schedule.

Again, most stakeholders couldn't care less about activities and Gantt charts and PERTs, but they do care about the project *deliverables* that help meet their expectations and *when* those deliverables will be delivered.

Identifying Stakeholders

Not every stakeholder will have the same degree of interest in the project and its outcomes, and the project plan won't necessarily include deliverables that speak to the expectations of *everyone* in the project stakeholder community, but it would be negligent of a PM not to at least identify all of these stakeholders, and what they want, as an early step in project planning.

Stakeholder identification starts with a broad definition of the word *stakeholder* and a stack of Post-it® notes. Pick one color to represent your stakeholders and stick with it; that way they'll stand out when you put them up on the wall. If you use blue, for example, everyone'll get used to thinking "stakeholder" when they see a blue Post-it® note on the wall.

Ask your project team to identify everyone and anyone who meets the definition of *stakeholder* (or do it yourself, if you want to kick-start the process), and write the name or role of one stakeholder on each Post-it® note. The obvious stakeholders will come thick and fast. The project sponsor is stakeholder number 1, of course, and people in the business lines who will be affected by the changes the project anticipates will also be mentioned early on.

Then go further: What about all the departments in the organization that will, to some extent, be involved in the project and have expectations of it? The IT group? Usually. Legal? Sure, if they're drafting or commenting on legal agreements associated with the project. Is your purchasing department a project stakeholder? Probably. Any vendors supplying the project? Yes. Finance? Absolutely—they'll have an interest in how the project is funded and paid for, whether it's capitalized or expensed and how.

Capitalizing and Expensing Project Costs

What portion of the money spent on your projects should be expensed (charged against earnings in the current year) and what part should get capitalized and depreciated over a longer period of time? The difference is really important. If you don't know the rules about what should get expensed and what should get capitalized on your project, get friendly with your neighborhood accounting folks fast. This will broaden your stakeholder engagement, which is always a good thing, but more pressing, budgeting isn't something that you want to mess up, and understanding expensing and capitalization might help you understand why some of your stakeholders act they way they do when it comes to project planning and project spending.

I've seen executives who want a team to hurry analysis of the appropriate solution—analysis being a phase in which costs can't be capitalized and will therefore affect earnings in the current period—and rush into the project itself, where costs *can* be capitalized and depreciated in the future.

Executives' desire to capitalize costs goes some way toward explaining why they might be hesitant to cancel a project that's well under way. Cancellation might mean that any dollars they'd planned to capitalize would have to then be expensed, creating expenses that weren't in their plans.

I've oversimplified here for effect, but the message should be clear: Understand which project (or preproject planning) costs are going to be expensed and which ones are going to be capitalized.

Figure 11.1 shows some (and only some; your list will be more comprehensive) of the typical stakeholders (in no particular order, except that the sponsor is always first) for a system implementation project that will involve changes to the way a company handles customer feedback on their product in compliance with new federal legislation. Each unique stakeholder group should be listed on a Post-it® note.

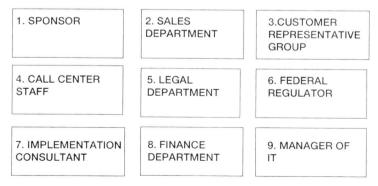

Figure 11.1 Possible Project Stakeholders

A rule of thumb here: If you end up with more than seven distinct and important stakeholder groups after you've done your consolidation of stakeholders, you've probably got a complex project on your hands. Lots of stakeholders with lots of expectations? That says *complex* to me.

How complex a project is isn't just about how big it is, how expensive it is, or how many people there are on the project team. As a matter of fact, the number of people involved and how much is being spent aren't nearly as good indicators of complexity as is the number of distinct stakeholder communities you're going to have to deal with. The more stakeholder communities with their own expectations of the project, the more complex the project, the more potential for conflicting expectations, and the more likely that the PM will have to spend even more time on communication.

Consolidating Stakeholders

Once you've identified all of your stakeholders, you'll probably want to do some consolidation. Twenty-five stakeholder communities (and it's not hard to identify 25 stakeholders on a project of any decent size and complexity) probably doesn't mean 25 unique sets of expectations. Stakeholders with common expectations can probably be managed as a group.

Example: You may have identified both your organization's CIO and IT manager of infrastructure as separate stakeholders. They may be, if they have differing sets of expectations, but you may be able to combine them if their expectations are the same.

CIO: "I know that Joe (the manager of infrastructure) is looking to ensure that whatever gets installed onto our network complies with our corporate standard infrastructure model—no weird network configurations, no Macs, nothing that doesn't use our standard middleware configuration, all right?"

PM: "So, you're telling me that if we recognize his expectations in the plan—if we put a couple of deliverables in the plan that involve him signing off on technical infrastructure pieces before we make any decisions to buy anything—that'll reflect your expectations for the project too?"

CIO: "That's exactly what I'm saying. Aside from those measures of success—those 'How do we know we've won?' answers you're always going on about—I'm saying that if you keep Joe happy, I'm happy."

In this case, you can probably combine two of your stakeholder Post-its® (one for the CIO and one for the IT manager of infrastructure) on to a single Post-it® note called, perhaps, "IT management."

Another example: Once you've laid out your stakeholder community on the Post-it® notes, you may find that you've gone crazy identifying management stakeholders. Not only have you got a Post-it® for the VP of marketing (your sponsor, in this case), you've also got one for the president (his boss), one for the board of directors, one for the chairman of the board, and even one representing the company's public shareholders. Legitimate stakeholders all, but probably not all unique stakeholder communities.

Ask yourself this question: If you keep your sponsor happy—that is, deliver the deliverables that meet his expectations for the project—does that mean that his bosses (the president, board, board chair, and shareholders) will also be satisfied?

If you can't identify a distinct and separate set of expectations for each of the stakeholders above your sponsor, you can probably combine them into a single stakeholder group called "senior management" or even, and more specifically and more descriptively, "all executive management from the sponsor up."

By considering the common expectations of stakeholders, you'll probably be able to reduce the number of unique stakeholder communities on your project considerably. But be careful not to do this too quickly or without checking your assumptions with the stakeholders first because you may be missing some unique expectations you hadn't fully considered.

Connecting Stakeholder Expectations to Specific Deliverables

With your stakeholder community documented, you can now focus on the important part: identifying the expectations for those stakeholders, making sure they don't conflict (if they do, you should bring your sponsor into the discussion), and identifying the specific deliverables your project will have to deliver to meet those expectations.

Now, put some structure around the information you've collected. Number all of the stakeholders, all of their expectations, and all of the deliverables. A numbering system will allow you to track the deliverables, the expectations that drove them, and the stakeholders who had those expectations. This will help you identify, for example, which stakeholders you should contact if a deliverable is going to be late.

Generally speaking, I put the most important stakeholder groups to the left (those that have the expectations that will drive the key project deliverables), starting with the sponsor as stakeholder number 1. This list of stakeholders, and their expectations and the subsequent deliverables that'll meet those expectations, make up what Dr. Francis Hartman calls a *stakeholder breakdown structure* (SBS). The highest level of a stakeholder breakdown structure for a natural gas drilling project might look like the one shown in Figure 11.2.

Figure 11.2 The Top Level of a Stakeholder Breakdown Structure

Once the project stakeholders have been identified, you're ready to invite them (most definitely including your sponsor) into your planning, so they can tell you what they're expecting from the project.

Generally speaking, the sponsor's expectations and required deliverables are pretty straightforward—they'll be represented by the project's "won" deliverables. If your project delivers all the "won" deliverables, subject to cost and schedule constraints, of course, you should expect to see a satisfied sponsor. Don't take this for granted, though. Take the opportunity to canvass the sponsor again in a planning session, just like you're going to do for the rest of the stakeholders: "Ms. Sponsor, beyond the 'won' deliverables, are there any other specific expectations that we should be planning deliverables for?" You may find that they do have some additional expectations.

For the rest of the stakeholders, what's the first and best piece of advice about understanding their expectations? Ask them. Publicly. In front of as many other stakeholders as you can. Invite them into your planning: Schedule a morning or afternoon working session to which you invite as many of the stakeholders (or their delegates, if you must) as you can.

In the session, remind the stakeholders what you're trying to do. (Of course, you have already sent out an agenda in advance so they know what's up and called each one personally to ask them to attend, haven't you?) Your goal is to identify what the stakeholders need and expect from the project so you can identify the deliverables that'll meet their expectations, determine if they have expectations the project can't fulfill, and invite their active participation in the meeting and in the broader project.

There's a side benefit here, too: When members of your stakeholder community meet and get to see what other stakeholders are looking for, you'll foster some good cross-stakeholder learning and understanding. (The IT guy might say to the finance guy: "I've always wondered why you finance guys want these projects to deliver a capital versus expense breakdown.")

In the session, ask the stakeholders to grab a set of Post-its® (a different color from the stakeholder Post-its®, to differentiate the *expectations* from the *stakeholders*), and write down, in simple sentences or point form, their expectations for the project, one on each Post-it®. It's a good idea to ask them to write with a thick black marker so the expectations can be read from across the room by everybody else who's involved in the planning.

Let's talk about what an important stakeholder (number 2, for example), the owner of the surface land off of which we would be drilling for natural gas—a rancher with a couple of hundred head of cattle on his property—might be looking for. Even though the rancher himself couldn't join us for the planning session, the landman from our company, whom he'd dealt with, could take a pretty good guess at what he was looking for.

"Two things," said the landman. "Money and land reclamation—like every other landowner in the area, he'll want a good-sized check before he lets our rig roll onto his property. And he'll want to ensure that when we're finished drilling and we move that rig back off again, that we put his land back in the same condition as it was before we got there."

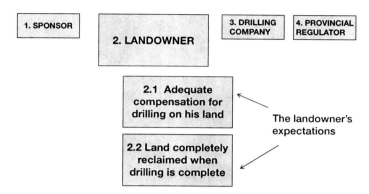

Figure 11.3 Mapping Stakeholder Expectations

Two expectations: adequate compensation for drilling on his land and land reclamation. Now we were getting somewhere. I captured them in a diagram similar to Figure 11.3.

The next question to ask: What deliverables will meet these expectations? The landman had an answer here, too.

"The going rate for access for the time we're going to be there is $30,000. Give him a check for $30K before the rig rolls, and he'll be fine."

"What about the reclamation stuff?" I asked.

"The provincial government has biologists or consultants who can do that kind of thing. We pay the fee, they'll come out and inspect the land before and after the drilling, take some soil samples, and assuming we haven't done anything stupid, they'll issue something called an LRC, or Land Reclamation Certificate."

"And that'll work for him?"

"Should be everything he needs," the landman said.

So I added that information to the stakeholder breakdown structure, making an explicit connection between the stakeholder (2), his expectations (2.1 and 2.2), and the specific project deliverables that would meet those expectations (2.1.1 and 2.2.1), as shown in Figure 11.4.

Now it was a matter of ensuring these deliverables found a place in the project schedule. Better yet, if those deliverables were delayed at all, my numbering system would tell me which stakeholder I needed to talk to about it—in this case, my stakeholder number 2, the landowner.

But we weren't finished with this stakeholder yet. Because he wasn't at the planning session, we thought we'd better confirm our plans with him. The landman and I met with him in the front room of his sprawling ranch house, and over a cup of coffee, we told him what we'd been up to.

"Thanks for meeting with us," I said. "This is an important project for us, and since we're going to be drilling on your property, it's important that we're lined up with what you're looking for." I unrolled the SBS on his table and showed him what we'd documented so far. "We're trying to make sure that

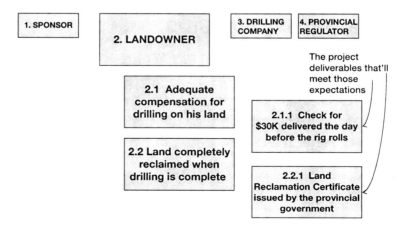

Figure 11.4 Aligning Deliverables with Stakeholder Expectations

we've captured everybody's expectations and that what we're delivering in the project meets those expectations."

"I appreciate you coming out, and I agree that it's better to be asking these questions now than three months into it," he said. When he'd looked over what we had, he said, "Well, you've got it mostly right—the access fee is right, and the LRC is good, but there's something else I'll need."

We asked what else he'd need to make the project work.

"Six months of advance notice on anything you're doing," he said. "My wife and I are snowbirds—we head down to Mesa, Arizona, every year late in October, and we don't come back until April. I know you want to be drilling in February [so that we could move the rig in and out over frozen ground], but I'll need to make sure that I have my son-in-law here while you're drilling. I'm all for your project, but not if I don't have anyone here looking out for my herd while your drilling crew is coming and going. And if I'm going to have him here, I'll have to give him six months' notice so he can make arrangements for his herd, too."

We hadn't expected that. Six months out was pretty far ahead in our planning for the level of detail he was looking for, but it was clear this was an expectation we'd have to meet because the rancher was a very important stakeholder. If we didn't do what he asked, we couldn't afford the delay, and we sure didn't want to be drilling the next summer.

The landman and I put our heads together and added the new expectation to our SBS then talked about what deliverables would meet the expectation. Here's what we came up with: We'd give the rancher a copy of our rolling schedule, including forecasts at least eight months out, and we'd send him a new copy with every update. Better than that, we came up with a couple of other deliverables to meet this new expectation:

- We arranged to meet with his son-in-law every two weeks when the rancher was away to review progress and ensure he was getting everything he needed. Because we were out at the drilling location regularly, it wasn't hard to add these meetings into the schedule.

- We also thought it would be a good idea to keep the rancher in the loop however we could, so we had our site superintendent take a picture of the project site every week and attach it to an email we had him send down to the rancher every week, which made our important stakeholder feel closer to the action—he could see the progress for himself.

Figure 11.5 shows how the landowner's additional expectation and the deliverables we added to the stakeholder breakdown structure.

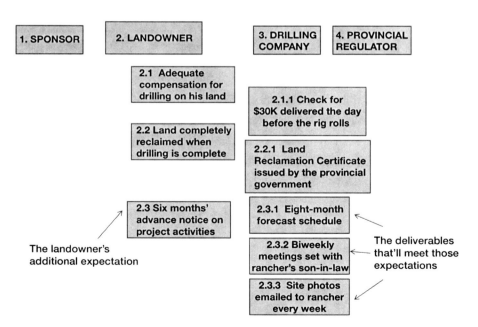

Figure 11.5 New Stakeholder Expectations and Matching Deliverables

Meeting with every stakeholder group on your project to elicit their expectations will go a long way toward two key objectives:

1. Ensuring that expectations you hadn't planned for don't pop up later. Even if they do, you've done your homework, and change requests to address these expectations won't be dismissed with, "You should have picked up on this in the first place."

2. Showing your project stakeholders the deliverables that meet their expectations in your 3D schedule (see Chapter 12). Instead of looking at a Gantt or PERT that means nothing to them and hoping that what they're looking for is somewhere in it, they'll be able to see and track the deliverables that are meaningful to them.

This method is a deliberate departure from the accidental and approximate way stakeholders are usually managed in projects. Explicitly identifying stakeholders and what they're expecting from the project, then articulating and planning for a specific set of deliverables to meet these expectations are key elements of an effectively managed project.

Responding to Conflicting Stakeholder Expectations

This is where an SBS is really helpful. If you haven't noticed conflicting or misaligned expectations up to this point, they'll be right there in front of you on the SBS.

You've deliberately and explicitly asked all project stakeholders to tell you what they're looking for, and in the process, you've made it much more difficult for stakeholders to keep hidden agendas hidden. With the explicit support of the project sponsor, you're making a deliberate effort to engage all the stakeholders to ensure that they're heard and understood.

If all of your stakeholders are given every opportunity to share their expectations early on, they'll look disingenuous revealing additional expectations later, and your sponsor can help manage these kinds of expectations. Resolving these kinds of conflicts is the sponsor's job and one of the reasons the role is so important to the success of the project. Even if some expectations are genuinely new and weren't hidden when you were doing the stakeholder-expectations exercise, having the SBS to refer to gives you the backup you need to trigger a legitimate change request:

"When we—you and I, Mr. Stakeholder-with-a-previously-unmentioned-expectation—worked on the SBS before, that expectation didn't come up, so we didn't identify deliverables to meet it, and therefore we don't have those deliverables in the plan. I'd be glad to look at this new expectation and define, with your agreement, the deliverable or deliverables to meet it. Then we'll put a change request together, reflecting the cost, schedule, or performance impact of this deliverable or deliverables, and you and I can take it to the sponsor for approval."

Better yet, the SBS makes it easy for your sponsor to be as supportive as they should be. Imagine this conversation between your project's very effective sponsor (see Chapter 8 for more on what makes an effective sponsor) and the project-hosting organization's CIO after you've done a thorough job of stakeholder evaluation and canvassing stakeholder expectations:

Sponsor: "Hanley says that something's come up from your IT team that we might not be able to address in the project."

CIO: "Yeah, we understand that the project as communicated to him didn't anticipate running the system on the new version of the middleware we'll be installing this fall. We'd always assumed that making it work on our new middleware standard would be part of the plan."

Sponsor: "Did he ask you about it?"

CIO: "Well, he did with that stakeholder analysis/breakdown structure/expectations thing we did when they were putting the first cut at the plan together."

Sponsor: "Did you talk about the new middleware requirement then?"

CIO: "No, we didn't... we were just kicking around the idea at that point—it probably would have been premature to discuss it then."

Sponsor: "So what's the issue?"

CIO: "Hanley's looking for an additional $100K and six weeks on to the project schedule to test the system against the new middleware, and he's asking me to support that change request."

Sponsor: "Isn't that reasonable?"

CIO: "Not unreasonable, I suppose, but we'd assumed that any additional costs would come out of the baseline project budget, not from additional funding."

Sponsor: "He asked for IT's expectations at the beginning, and no one from your shop said that this requirement was something they needed up front, and we set the budget and schedule accordingly. I can't see what's wrong with his need for a change request. I think you and I should both be supporting the change request if you think running on the new middleware is really important."

Of course, the sponsor—assuming they are a *genuine* sponsor, empowered to make the final decision on behalf of the organization—may say no to the change request (and this is the sponsor's decision, as part of their active role in the project), or they may agree to incorporate this additional expectation, which you can handle through a disciplined change-control process. (But remember: Changes are *never* free. See Chapter 21.)

CHAPTER 12

DROP DEAD DATE (3D) SCHEDULING

It pays to be obvious, especially if you have a reputation for subtlety.

—Isaac Asimov

PERTs, Gantts, and critical paths make lots of sense to us project managers, trained in their use as we are, but they don't mean much to most of our project stakeholders. They don't care much about them, and more importantly, they *shouldn't* care much about them.

Being an effective PM is not about showing how smart you are ("See these cool PM tools and techniques I know how to use because I'm a Project Management Professional? Don't you wish you knew how to use them, too?"); it's all about how effectively you can communicate what needs to be communicated.

So what does your project schedule really need to communicate? How about:

- Major project milestones and when they need to be achieved to keep the schedule on track
- The major deliverables (*not* the activities required to get there) at each milestone that will tell the reader whether or not the project team has achieved the milestone

- Who is responsible for the major deliverables at each milestone

- Progress toward those major milestones.

These are the things your stakeholder community really cares about. Stakeholders really don't care about successor and predecessor activities and velocities and activities that roll up, and they really don't want you to shove this information down their throats in your attempt to communicate "effectively" about the project. Any representation of a project schedule and progress against it that needs to be explained in technical PM terms is not only ineffective but possibly damaging to your interests.

Drop dead date (3D) scheduling is a simpler alternative. A 3D schedule represents, at the highest level, the linear sequence of milestones that need to be achieved in order to make the schedule. Each milestone is complete when all of the project deliverables associated with the milestone are complete (see Figure 12.1). Complete all the deliverables associated with the milestone at or before the milestone date, and you're on track. If you don't make the required deliverables before or at the milestone date, you're late. A 3D schedule contains exactly the information you want to communicate in the way that you should be communicating it—as a high-level representation of the sequence of major events (see Figure 12.2).

Think of 3D as latest-possible-date scheduling. Each milestone is, in fact, a dropdead date. You may finish delivera-

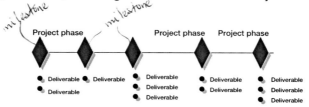

Figure 12.1 The Structure of a Drop Dead Date (3D) Schedule

Figure 12.2 A 3D Schedule in Use for a Telecommunications Project

bles before the scheduled dates, but you can't finish any later if you want to make the milestone (see Figure 12.3). Some deliverables may come earlier than the milestone date they're associated with; some may in fact *need* to be completed earlier. The 3D isn't intended to show the sequence of deliverables that need to be completed, it just shows the latest date they can be completed without pushing out the overall schedule. Deliver late on any deliverable that's necessary to claim a milestone, and you're behind. Miss by a day, and without any other intervention (such as adding more resources or changing scope, quality, or both), the end date of the project will move out at least one day for every day late in achieving the milestone.

A 3D schedule doesn't show slack, and it certainly doesn't include contingency. You either make all the deliverables at or

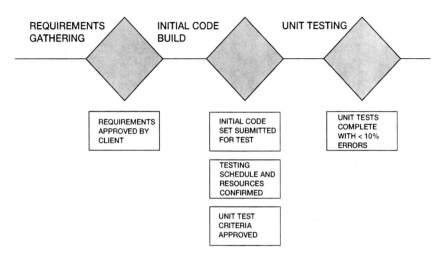

Figure 12.3 Deliverables at Milestones

before the scheduled milestone date, or you're late. Showing slack at this level is unnecessary and invites abuse. Discussing slack with people who don't understand the intricacies of our PM tools is pointless and dangerous, almost as dangerous as putting contingency in your schedule, which is often misunderstood and abused in the same way.

This direct one-to-one focus on milestones tends to focus attention on them. Drop dead date scheduling isn't exactly critical path, but it may as well be. (*Critical path* is another one of those PM terms that is badly misunderstood by non-PM professionals.) The 3D method is simpler.

Below the level of a 3D schedule, and especially when managing details between 3D milestones, you may want to run a Gantt or a PERT that shows sequence details and dependencies. These tools may be necessary for you to manage at your level, but they're a lousy way to communicate with the broad stakeholder community. Stakeholders want to see progress against major milestones; they don't want to have to learn to read and interpret Gantts and PERTs. I won't go into Gantts and PERTs and such in any more detail here; suffice it to say that they're useful tools for managing large and complex projects with many activities and interdependencies, but you shouldn't use them to communicate with anyone else.

Chapter 13

Measuring All the Way Through

We've talked about defining a set of deliverables that indicate a successful project (the "wons") at the point that the project is "done," as well as the critical importance of identifying those deliverables up front. Now we come to another oft-neglected element of project management: determining effective interim measures of progress against those ultimate goals.

Interim measurement is much more than just simply reporting on progress against schedule and budget. We've all seen projects that are tracking on budget and seem to be delivering the (ill-defined) stuff they said they'd deliver but are otherwise complete disasters. And that's because, in the absence of other metrics, budget and schedule adherence are seen as proxies for project success: "We haven't exceeded the budget yet, and we seem to be finishing our activities on time; we must be successful at this point, right?"

Not quite. Budget and schedule are inadequate indicators of progress toward the real reasons that projects are undertaken. They're not undertaken to stay on or under budget or to stay on schedule; they're taken on for specific purposes for the organizations that host them, purposes with readily measurable outcomes (we hope).

I remember being four months into a ten-month project and a client CEO saying to me: "Look, I really don't care about the details—that's your job—and your reporting just isn't doing it for me. Just telling me that we're on budget and schedule doesn't give me any real assurance; this project is all about giving us price transparency when we sell our big equipment and add-ons through our retailers. What can you show me right now—since we're spending a lot of money on this project right now—that indicates that we're making progress toward that goal?"

What executives who sponsor and fund projects are looking for are interim measures of progress against the identifiable end-point measures of success. If you say, for example, that you're going to reduce average call-handling time from more than four minutes to less than two minutes as a result of a new call-center support system, how will you know, as the project rolls along, that you're making tangible progress toward that goal?

In the case of the call-center support system, we decided to pilot the new system in three eastern states during the project, aiming to test the system and its capacity before go-live, and we thought that we should get some feedback on performance given the volume of calls handled over the one-month pilot period in those three states. We asked ourselves three questions:

1. If reducing average call-handling time to less than two minutes is a measure of success at the end, will we be seeing any interim indicators before we go live that we're on track to achieve that reduction?
2. Will there be any interim measures of our success in cutting call-handling staff by 30 percent?
3. What interim metrics do we have to determine whether we've increased customer satisfaction?

When a CEO asks how the project is going six months in and after spending a million dollars, "It's going well," or "We're OK," or "Fine" are not acceptable answers. How do you know it's "going well" or "OK," and what does '"fine" mean? And that's what interim measures of performance are all about: identifying in advance the conditions that will tell you, me, or the questioning CEO that the project is progressing toward "won."

If we don't have any interim indicators of success (or of problems), we're essentially saying: "Trust us, even though we don't have anything to show you as we move through the project." This kind of suggestion makes me nervous, and it makes sponsoring executives nervous, too. When a PM says this, we hear, "We really won't know if the $10 million dollars you've entrusted us with will deliver what we're aiming for until the whole project is nearly done, after we've spent almost the entire $10 million and we flip the switch to turn on the new system." Yikes.

Projects lack real interim measures for two reasons:

1. ***They really don't*** have ***any good interim indicators of performance.*** For some projects, we just won't know for sure that it "worked" until we flip the switch at go-live. If we won't have any real interim performance indicators as we progress, nothing to really measure until we're finished, we owe it to our clients to be absolutely clear about this up front: "We've tried, but we can't identify any interim measures of success for this project. We really won't know if it worked until we're finished." This kind of project represents, to an extent, risk capital. Whether or not the hosting organization is going to get the payoff anticipated won't be clear until the project is complete.

2. ***An oversight on the part of PMs.*** We're either not looking for interim measures of project performance, we're not reporting on them, or both. If they do exist, we owe it to

our clients and our projects to measure and report on them, to answer the question, "If things are going well (or not so well) four months into a ten-month project, *how will we know?*" explicitly in our reporting.

Chapter 20 discusses checkpoints, the points during a project at which interim progress is measured, in detail.

CHAPTER 14

ESTIMATING (BETTER)

It is the mark of an instructed mind to rest satisfied with the degree of precision which the nature of the subject permits and not seek an exactness where only an approximation of the truth is possible.

—Aristotle

As project managers, we live and die by estimates. And as important as accurate estimating is to us, we don't do a very good job of it, mostly, I think, because we tend to forget what the word *estimate* means. That's the thing about estimates: They're just that. The word *estimate*, by its very nature, implies a degree of uncertainty, implies a range of possible outcomes. Estimates represent approximate judgements; they reflect best guesses, absent certainty. So a single-point estimate ("We think it'll take 40 person-days of work effort to get it done") isn't very helpful at all; I'd even argue that it's an oxymoron. And it doesn't say anything about our level of comfort with the number we're providing. ("What I really should have said is that it could take anywhere *between* 20 and 60 days of work effort to get it done.")

More dangerous, because of the way we tend to present these single-point estimates, they lead to an illusion of precision. Have you ever seen an estimate for a single piece of work, or worse yet, an entire project, that looks something like this?

Estimate: $108,870

And sometimes it's made worse by tacking pennies onto the end.

I'd bet that if you tracked down the perpetrator (*perpetrator* is a good word, given how much bad estimates can hurt us) of this estimate and asked them how they came up with the number, they'd likely say something like this:

"I didn't mean to imply precision, of course—everyone understands that, don't they? That estimate's just an average unit cost of time multiplied by an estimated number of hours, like this:

- We *estimate* 950 hours of programming time

- The *average* cost for an hour of programming time is $114.60

- Therefore, 950 hours x $114.60/hour = $108,870.

An estimate. Nothing more than that."

Unfortunately, that's not how our clients and sponsors see it. They reason that because we've done this kind of work before (we *are* experienced project managers, after all), we must know *exactly* what we're doing and *exactly* how long it'll take, especially since we've got the estimate down to the dollar (or to the 870 dollars, in this case).

The estimator, of course, would be horrified to find that their number was being read that way, but they may find that their own marketing people have already committed to it on a fixed-price basis (this *never* happens in real life, does it?) to accommodate the client's preordained expectations: "We know that you only budgeted $100,000 for this work," the marketing people will say. "I'm sure our team will do everything they can to get it in under 100K."

And what's worse? Your client will tend to remember the *earliest date* and the *lowest cost* they ever hear, regardless of whether that date or price is qualified with "given the following assumptions" or "over this range of possibilities."

Accuracy assumed. Unrealistic expectations set. The lesson? It's critical that we understand and communicate that a level of accuracy below the thousands (or even tens of thousands) of dollars (or tens or hundreds of hours) can't begin to emerge until *after* detailed planning is complete, and even that depends on how much you and your sponsors are willing to invest in planning and analysis.

So we have estimates that aren't really seen as estimates and estimates that set unrealistic expectations. What to do about it?

Describe Uncertainty in Understandable Terms

When we're talking about the uncertainty associated with an estimate, we'll always do well to talk in terms that make the most sense to the person we're talking to. And that means *not* talking about things we don't know enough about yet, like "work effort for requirements gathering" or "programmer hours per function point."

To illustrate: After a frustrating morning meeting talking about a new project the VP of marketing was proposing, the CEO and I sat down over lunch. "How come you IT guys can never seem to give us firm numbers?" he asked. "There's always a lot of hemming and hawing when we try to pin IT down on a schedule or a budget. Haven't you guys been doing systems for years? Shouldn't this be old hat by now?"

I knew what he was referring to: a C class estimate that the IT team had put forward in the morning meeting—*C class* meaning that the team didn't know much about the project, so it put forward a schedule and budget that reflected its uncertainty. In this case, the numbers it offered were to be considered accurate within −50% to + 100% for both cost and work effort.

The team (wisely and bravely, I think) put these numbers on the table because it had very little opportunity to analyze and estimate for the project and because marketing's project idea had only been described in a very general and not-very-detailed way. So how could I make this uncertainty real to the CEO?

"Bob," I said, "how much would it cost you to open a new retail location?"

He thought about it for a moment. "Where would we be opening? Costs vary considerably by province. And how big a location are we talking about? Are we talking about a full-service store or one of our satellite branches? Are we talking about opening in a mall or in a standalone building?"

I paused for effect, then said, "I don't know any of those things yet, but I still want you to give me an accurate budget estimate, right now."

He got the point.

"I don't mean to be difficult," I continued, "but we do need to understand how much we *don't* know at this point and what degree of variability that implies."

The things we *don't* know about projects make single-point estimates seem even more ridiculous. The more we know up front and the more time we spend in planning, the more accurate the estimate. We know this instinctively, but we're not very good at communicating it. For example, I know that if I want a new 2011 King Ranch Ford F-150 4x4, configured exactly the same way my neighbor's is, I can get exactly what I want for \$44,137 plus taxes. Ask yourself: Are you being asked to provide an estimate for a "loaded 2011 King Ranch Ford F-150 4x4," or for "some form of transportation that we can run on the highway?"

In any case, use comparisons and analogies that the people asking for the estimate will understand, and help them to understand the degree of uncertainty you're dealing with, also in terms they'll understand.

Never Start Your Plan with an End Date in Mind

I know this sounds odd because so often we start projects with mandated end dates (which, I'll cynically suggest, are too often set even before we know what we're really doing). Too often, we hear, "This product has to be market ready by March 1, or we'll lose the first-mover advantage," or "The new legislation takes effect on June 1, and we have to be in a position to comply with regulatory reporting requirements by then." But this *doesn't* mean the end date should have any part in our first-cut planning.

I'll argue that tying a first plan to a predetermined end date leads to all kinds of unreasonable estimates. It's amazing to me how much *we think* we can fit into a project when we know the deadline before we've done any planning work.

Watch an experienced construction project manager at work. One of the first things the good ones will do is flip to the *last* activities on the plan, to understand how realistic those last activities look, before they'll pass judgment on the likelihood of you making your end date. They've learned from hard experience that people (yes, you and I) tend to cram the last project activities into their schedules to finish by a planned date, even if they don't realize they're doing it.

Want to know how realistic your end dates are on an IT project? Ask your testing manager, the person who starts their work after everyone else is finished; the one responsible for some of the last big tasks on the project; the one who has to live with all the sins, shortcomings, and delays of the activities that came before. If the testing manager thinks your testing activities are unnecessarily compressed to meet a (predetermined) end date, listen closely. They know that any delays will mean that their tight testing activities will be further squeezed by any delay in predecessor activities.

> *This is not a novel to be tossed aside lightly. It should be thrown with great force.*
>
> —Dorothy Parker

I want project teams to understand that the first set of plans they put together should be all about what needs to be done to meet the "done" and "won" criteria and that date constraints should be tossed aside with great force the first time through. Let me say that again: The first plan should focus on what needs to be done to achieve the goals of the project, absent the constraint of dates. Yes, yes, dates are critical, and often they can't be moved, but if you start with the dates in mind, I can almost guarantee you and your team will compress all your activities to fit the date you have.

So run the first set of plans to meet the deliverables you must make to be successful. Take a look at the work effort required to deliver and then apply the resources you've got—that'll give you a suggested end date. If it turns out the end date you're coming up with is later than the "required" date (and it often is), you can now use a deliberate and disciplined process in your second planning pass that looks at what compromises you'll have to make in scope, quality, or both, or what resources you'll have to add, to meet the required date.

Bottom line: Plan for the *deliverables* without thinking about the end date the first time through, and *then* look at the changes you'll have to make to hit a preestablished date. You'll get a much more realistic assessment of what you need to do to meet that date.

Base Estimates on Past Experience

It's remarkable how quickly we forget about what's happened in the past when we're planning for the future. This must be part of some primal coping mechanism in human beings: If some mothers recalled the sleepless early nights with their first child, they'd never have a second. More simply: Those of us who don't learn from the past are destined to repeat it, and, man, we PMs too often do.

The volume of historic project data we have access to today is unprecedented. If we're insisting, as we should, that all of our projects incorporate project closeout reviews that are then made available to other project teams, and if we're doing our tracking right, we should be able to pull reams of data on historical project performance to look at and learn from. Providing and analyzing this information for project teams, by the way, is a very valuable role that could be played by the Project Management Office (PMO).

Even though we can learn so much from what's happened in the past, it seems we're still making the same dumb (usually overly optimistic) estimating mistakes we've been making since the building of the ancient pyramids. To wit: In spite of everything we've learned about estimating for project budgets and schedules/durations, we still insist on estimating projects based on the lowest (completely unreasonable) budget and the earliest (entirely laughable) date that anyone ever mentions.

We either advocate for these unrealities ourselves, or we let them be imposed on us. In either case, the behavior is inexcusable.

We know in our guts and from hard experience how wildly optimistic first estimates tend to be, especially when we really don't understand the entire problem we're dealing with, which is almost always the case when first estimates are being put together. We should know better: There is data out there that tells us about typical project performance, and excellent organizations like the Software Engineering Institute are doing some good work in this area. Even without looking outside of our own organizations, we should be able to come up with some more accurate estimates for the future based on what's happened to us in the past (here, again, the PMO should be able to help us).

So go pull up the records on the last five projects your organization has taken on (don't tell me you're not keeping track of this stuff—if not, you've got another problem from the past that you need to fix), and write down their original estimates for cost and duration. Then find out what the final price and duration for these projects were, assuming they weren't cancelled. Pretty scary, eh? Forget about trying to account for changes in scope or excuses for delay, just write the original estimates down beside the actual outcomes, and then do some simple math: On a percentage basis, how did the actuals play out against first estimates? Maybe the cost actuals averaged 150 percent of the first estimates. What about duration? Maybe the projects lasted, on average, 160 percent as long as first estimates. And then take a look at the first estimates for the new project you've got coming up, and tell me why, this time, the actual cost won't be 150 percent of the first estimate and why the duration of this one won't be 160 percent of what you first thought.

"It's the learning curve," I've heard.

"We're more experienced now," I've heard.

Yeah, right. That and four and a quarter will get you a venti cappuccino at Starbucks.

When project budgets and schedules are presented to me now, I always ask: "Why should this project be any closer to the original estimates than any others we've taken on?" And unless I hear some specific reasons why our estimating has got better, why should I assume this one is going to be different?

There's a bunch of fundamental stuff in our business that we can fix, stuff from the past such as estimating, stuff that's been plaguing us for years, and now that we've got the information we need to attack the problem, there's no excuse not to. Learn from the past or be doomed to repeat it.

Use Estimate Ranges and Associated Estimate Classes

As we discussed earlier in this chapter, single-point estimates imply precision, and they shouldn't unless you can explicitly communicate the uncertainty that the estimate implies somewhere in the estimate number itself. A conversation I recall from a couple of years back:

CFO: "Ken, we need to put a placeholder in next year's budget for that ERP thing we were talking about yesterday, and I need to have the budget submitted by 4:30 tomorrow. What number should I use?"

Me: "Well, it's not that simple... without some more analysis, any number I give you won't be any more than a SWAG."

CFO: "A what?"

Me: "A SWAG—a 'scientific wild-ass guess.' Look, you've given me one day, and I can't give you any kind of realistic estimate without some analysis."

CFO: "No one's going to hold you to the number you give me, but I do need something to put into the budget book."

And you know the rest of the story—I presented a SWAG, and it was loaded into the budget book. Nowhere in the budget book did the words "Be very careful: This is a SWAG" appear, and there never was an agreement on how much of a guess the G in SWAG represented. Once it got into the book, however, it took on a gravity and assumption of precision it never should have, and it would have been worse the more precise the number looked—for example, $108,870.

The starting point in fixing this problem is coming to an agreement on estimate classes. I suggest you start with something like this:

C Class Estimates

A C class estimate is the equivalent of a SWAG. It reflects a dollar amount or completion date that, given what we know and don't know, we should expect to be accurate within –50 percent to + 100 percent. What we're communicating through a C class estimate is that we really don't have enough information to provide a more accurate estimate; making a more accurate estimate would be, I'd argue, irresponsible at this point.

If I make a C class cost estimate of $1,000,000 (note that I'm deliberately suggesting a round number), we should all expect the *actual* number, when the project is finished, to fall somewhere between $500,000 (–50 percent) and $2,000,000 (+100 percent). If we're unhappy with that level of uncertainty, we know that we'll have to invest the time and money in getting to a more accurate estimate, one that is B or A class.

B Class Estimates

A B class estimate says that we've done a little bit of analysis/ sizing work, and we know a little bit more about this project— certainly more than we'd need to know to make a SWAG—or that we're proposing to do something we've done before and know a few things about. A B class estimate should be accurate within −25 percent and +50 percent. So if we estimate the total cost of a project at $800,000, we should all expect the *actual* number when it's completed to come in somewhere between $600,000 (−25 percent) and $1,200,000 (+50 percent).

A Class Estimates

An A class estimate indicates that we've done a bunch of work in narrowing the numbers down—in fact, we've probably built a fairly detailed plan to get down to this level of expected accuracy—and we can expect the number or date we put forward to be accurate within −15 percent to +25 percent. If our estimated budget is $850,000, we should all expect the *actual* number for the completed project to come in somewhere between about $725,000 (about 15 percent under the estimate; remember that we're trying not to mistakenly communicate too much preci- sion) and about $1,100,000.

Estimate classes in your organization may be tighter than the three I've proposed above, especially if there is more certainty and repeatability in the projects you do. The classes your organ- ization uses are up to you and your management. The estimate ranges you choose to use will depend on:

- *The type of project you're estimating.* If it's a software development or new product research project, you're inventing something new, so you should expect a wider range of estimate classes. Construction? If you want to build a building just like the one you built last year, I'd expect to see a narrower set of estimate ranges.

- *How much relevant historical data you have to look at.* Do you have records of how much effort was needed or how much it cost to do something like this before?

Even when estimate classes are used rigorously and in a disciplined manner, we still have the problem of how we communicate the estimate class associated with every number we present. I'm betting that your CFO's budget spreadsheet probably doesn't have a column for "estimate class associated with this number." Take heart—there is a way to ensure that an estimate and the degree of uncertainty associated with that estimate stick together.

Communicating the Level of Uncertainty

Looking at a client's material take off (MTO) for a gas plant upgrade a couple of years back, what appeared at first to be either a remarkable degree of precision or an incredible coincidence turned out to be neither. Instead, it revealed a clear and concise way to communicate the range of certainty (or uncertainty) associated with cost estimates. Here's what I saw:

- Electrical and instrumentation material $2,000,000.77
- Piping and insulation material $3,500,000.88
- Structural steel and fabrication material $5,000,000.77
- Foundation, pad, and support material $1,500,000.88

I said, "Estimates down to the penny... that's quite an impressive level of accuracy. And the fact that all those numbers end in .77 or .88—that's quite a coincidence."

The PM said, "They aren't particularly accurate, in fact, and the numbers aren't a coincidence. What they are is an explicit communication of the degree of uncertainty associated with those numbers and the range of accuracy that can be expected from them. We have three estimate classes: A, B, and C. For us, C means the number we're giving is expected to be accurate −25 percent to +50 percent, B means −15 percent to +20 percent, and A means −5 percent to +10 percent."

"Sounds good," I said, "but what's with the .77 and .88?"

"That's where the explicit communication part comes in," he said. "We put a .77 on any number that's a C class estimate, a .88 on any B class estimate, and a .99 on any A class estimate."

The beauty of the thing took a minute to sink in.

"What it means," he continued, "is that no one in this organization, from the CEO down to the most junior programmer, has any misconception about the degree of uncertainty associated with the numbers we put out there. Everybody knows the estimate classes, and everybody knows what the .77s and .88s and .99s mean. There's no confusion, and no one can pretend they don't understand the risk and uncertainty we're dealing with. We talk a lot about what we have to do to get more accurate estimates and what we're willing to invest to get them, but we've gotten past the confusion and unrealistic expectations."

I suggest you try something along the same lines.

CHAPTER 15

PROJECT RISK: THE BROAD STROKES

Here's the thing about project risk management: Every PM knows they need to be doing it, and almost every PM takes a stab at it one way or another, but they all seem to struggle with *connecting* risk management with how they plan and manage their projects—connecting it in a disciplined, organized, yes-we-can-see-the-impact-of-deliberate-risk-management-throughout-the-entire-project kind of way.

Sure, teams meet about risks, create long lists of risks, and spend hours talking about risk mitigation, but these meetings often end in broad generalizations: "Well, we'll just have to make sure that these things don't happen on this project, won't we?" And so we get "risk words" on a whiteboard or a flip chart, or even in the documented minutes of the meeting, and we end up with risk management artifacts that... mean what, exactly? These artifacts—these we're-not-sure-what-to-do-with-them risk management artifacts—float around on the periphery of the project, reminding us of their presence from time to time, reminding us that we really *should* be doing something more specific and deliberate. And then they start to look like that annoying cousin you only see once in a while, the one who turns up once a year because your mom insists that you invite him to your birthday party. When he's there, you know he's there, you're just not sure what to do with him. And so the process of managing project risk stays somewhat disconnected from everything else on the project. Sure, you've got a list of risks and some ideas about what to do about them and what you should be doing with them, but that's about it.

Done well, risk management isn't something that's *added on* to a project; it's something that's *built into* it every step of the way. Here's what you do with risk management: deep integration. A deep integration of risk management into every part of your project—into the planning and into the estimating, into the management and into the measurement and reporting, and into the way you close out projects. At the most basic, it's a six-step process:

1. Risk identification
2. Risk categorization and scheduling
3. Risk mitigation
4. Risk management
5. Risk reporting
6. Risk closeout.

A Quick Word about Words: Risk, Event, and Risk Mitigations

The terminology surrounding risk and risk management can be confusing. For the purposes of this book:

- A *risk* is something that might happen—for example, there is a risk that the new piece of software we need for development won't be delivered by the software manufacturer in time, which would have a negative impact on our schedule and budget.

- A *risk event* is when a risk actually happens. The late delivery of a critical server is a risk; if the server is in fact delivered late, it becomes a risk event.

- *Risk mitigations* are put in place to ensure the risks we identify don't turn into risk events or to make sure the impact of risk events is minimized.

CHAPTER 16

STEP 1: RISK IDENTIFICATION

Too often, risk identification is an informal process. We hold meetings (well *before* our project planning is completed, I trust) where all and sundry are asked to rack their brains for risks: "What are we worried about? What's hurt us in the past?" And we end up with lists of risks that are all over the map—some serious and needing immediate attention: "I'm worried that we're not going to be able to get enough time from the Data Base Administrator to load all the data sets we need in time for testing," and some seemingly trivial: "We might get hit by lightning."

The process of identifying risks, both serious and trivial, probable or unlikely, short term or all-project-long, should be better organized than it usually is, and better organization starts with knowing where to look for risks in the first place.

Hit by Lightning: Consider *All* the Risks

I learned a good lesson a few years back in a risk identification exercise: When you ask for people's input, it's critical to respect and capture and consider *all* input, regardless of how off the wall it might seem to be. We were identifying risks on a project to build the control sites for a remote-control natural gas gathering system. The sites would control the flow of gas into the local pipeline system. We'd been considering all kinds of risks—weather delays, equipment failures, and the potential for late deliveries—when one of the field operators, who hadn't said anything up to this point, said: "And we'd better have a backup plan if those sites get hit by lightning."

I was tempted, of course, to just put that one aside and not write it down. "That's pretty bloody unlikely," the voice in my head said. "Why would we even waste time looking at it?" Good thing the voice in my head stayed there; write it down I did, thinking it was better not to ignore any input offered, especially from the field guys on the team, who didn't talk much in any case.

And I'm glad I did. One of the engineers on the team caught me at the next break. "Glad we caught that lightning strike thing—I'd almost forgotten about that one." Before I could say anything, he continued: "Remember that we'll be building these things out in the middle of the bald prairie, with nothing around them for miles, and that means the receiving stations are going to be the tallest things around… until he [the field operator] mentioned it, I'd forgotten that our facilities out there took lightning strikes three times last summer."

Lesson learned: Pay attention to everything you hear, no matter how crazy it sounds at the time. The really unhelpful suggestions and the genuinely crazy ideas—the ones that aren't going to help you manage the project better—can be "managed out" later through a disciplined risk categorization process.

Yes, the probability of a lightning strike in most projects would be infinitesimal, and the PM could choose to reject this type of input right off the top. This approach would seem to save a step, but it would also mark the PM as the guy who rejected the input, the guy who doesn't always listen, the guy who doesn't take suggestions.

A better approach: Let the discipline in the process edit out extraneous or unhelpful ideas. The risk categorization process itself will filter them out. If the *team* agrees, as part of the *process*, that the chance of getting hit by lightning is of such a remote possibility that it doesn't make sense to invest in a strategy to mitigate the risk of getting hit by lightning, it's the *team* and the *process* making the call and not you, the "not listening" PM.

If someone on your team thinks you're not listening to them or anyone else, regardless of the ultimate value of what they're telling you, you can be pretty sure this person won't go out of their way to contribute later on, when you'll probably need their input the most.

Priming the Risk-Thinking Pump

Don't start with a blank page when identifying risks. That's always a tough place to start—you're bound to start too slowly or miss something important if you don't have a way to prime the "risk-thinking pump." Here are four questions that prime that pump.

Question 1: What Kinds of Bad Stuff Has Happened to Us on Past Projects?

Historical information is a really good place to start, and using it is one of the markers of a learning organization—an organization that knows enough not to make the same mistake twice. In addition to what the team itself knows about the past, the Project Management Office (ignoring, for a moment, that calling a potentially very useful group of people a *project management office* is a really dumb idea) can be really helpful; the (mandatory!) project closeout reports they've been diligently collecting are a great resource.

Ideally, the PMO should be able to offer something like this: "How about if we bring to the risk identification session a list of all the risks that other project teams here have identified, what they did to mitigate them, and how those mitigations worked out? And while we're at it, we've been gathering all the project closeout reports that we can find from other organizations, too, and we've created a list of project risks from them as well. Would that be helpful?" A good PM wouldn't be able to say "yes, please" fast enough. It's a safe assumption that the project being planned will have much in common with many projects that have come before it. Thinking "We're different" or "Our project is unique" represents a dangerous misunderstanding and the height of PM arrogance.

The First and Last Deliverables on *Any* Project: Closeout Reports

If you want to embed discipline in risk identification and mitigation into your projects, a careful review of previous project closeout reports should be the first—and mandatory—deliverable for every project you work on. Project closeouts are a valuable tool that allows project teams to learn from the past. If not every past project has been hugely successful, we need to pay attention to the reasons why they haven't.

Aside from the information they offer on past project risks, risk mitigations, and outcomes, well-written project closeout reports should be a source of all kinds of valuable data:

- How close were we to our estimates last time, and what does this say about our estimates this time?

- What assumptions did we make? Were they good assumptions? Did we miss any?

With closeout reports in hand, your project team should ask two questions:

1. What good things (always start with the good things) happened on previous projects, and what can we do to help these good things happen on this project, too?
2. What bad things happened on our projects before, and what can we do on this project to ensure they don't happen here?

Of course, you'll have to contribute to the body of close out information by completing a project closeout report for *your* project. If every project team completes a thorough closeout report focused on lessons learned and advice for the future, and every team reviews these closeout reports, asking, "What can we learn from the past, and how will this make our project better?" and all of this is supported by a diligent project performance center team that collects and shares the reports, you'll have a real learning project organization.

Question 2: What's Driving the Variability and Uncertainty in Our Three-Point Estimates?

Talking about the range of possibilities for our three-point estimates will yield a rich vein of risk-identification information. For example, a PM might say, "OK, now we all understand—

- The deliverables we'll have to produce to make milestone 3

- The deliverables we'll need to produce to make milestone 4
- The resources we'll have available to work on the deliverables between milestones 3 and 4.

Our three-point estimate for the phase between 3 and 4 says that the best-case duration is three weeks, likely-case duration is five weeks, and worst-case duration is ten weeks. What I want to know is: What are we worried about happening that could drive the duration for this phase out to ten weeks?"

Here's where risks begin to emerge. Just what *is* the team worried about that could take the duration of that phase out to ten weeks? The risks were probably already in the back of the team members' minds when they came up with the ten-week worst-case estimate, but they probably weren't captured at the time. Capture them now (see Figure 16.1).

Team member 1: "We could go to ten weeks if that server we ordered doesn't get up here and configured on time."

Team member 2: "And ten weeks sure isn't out of the question if we have the same kind of trouble stabilizing the test database that we had last time."

These are two potential risk events. So what are the risks that drive them?

Delay in getting development server set up will delay integration testing	Trouble stabilizing the test database	Language difficulties between domestic and India-based coders will result in missed requirements
Accounting SMEs will not have adequate time at month end to participate in testing	Competing projects on same server won't allow adequate code build time	

Figure 16.1 Typical Risk List for a Systems Development Project

PM: "So what could cause the server to be delayed? And why didn't the test database stabilize on schedule last time?"

In the answers lie the risks, the risks that'll get added to our risk list. Even more important for the risk *mitigations,* the PM should say, "What do you think we should do to make sure these things don't happen this time?"

Question 3: What Else Is the Team Worried About?

Discussing all possible risks is the "traditional" way risks are identified, and it shouldn't be overlooked. Maybe there are new concerns that haven't come up previously and aren't reflected in the estimate ranges. Ask and ask again, and add anything you haven't heard before, regardless of whether or not it makes sense to you at this point, to your risk list.

Question 4: What Do the Other Project Stakeholders Think about Risk to the Project?

Your stakeholders might see risks that you and your team do not, and this is another excellent opportunity to engage them. You did it when you were gathering stakeholder expectations and related deliverables when you started planning, and you do plan to keep the communication channels with them wide open throughout the whole project, don't you?

Here's a chance to use that powerful engagement statement again: "We need your help." In this case, ask for help from every stakeholder you can reach: "We need your help in identifying risks to the project, and we're going to do everything we can to mitigate those risks. Is there anything you can see that might have a negative impact on our schedule, on our budget, or on our performance?"

Even if your stakeholders haven't caught something you missed, they'll appreciate that you consulted them, you'll reinforce how important their active involvement in the project is, and you'll strengthen relationships that you're going to be counting on throughout the project.

Being Specific about Risks

Now that you've gathered a raw list of risks, it's time to get more information about them that will help you categorize them. The clearer and more explicit you can be about risks, the better. Long, explicit definitions of risks may be tougher to fit on a Post-it® note (see Chapter 17), but they'll go a long way toward ensuring that everyone on the team understands the same risks in the same way. It is tempting to use shorthand, especially when the risks are flying thick and fast during your risk identification meeting, but resist the temptation.

I've seen teams write vague things such as "the server" as a risk. Does this mean there is a risk that the server will fail? That it will be delivered or configured late? That it doesn't have the capacity to support the project? "The server" just isn't enough information. I've seen "weather" tagged as a risk on a construction project. That's not clear enough, either. Much better: "Risk that wet weather will delay access to the site for heavy equipment needed to set the foundations." That's a risk I can act on; it's easier to categorize, and I can develop a specific mitigation strategy. With risk management, more information is always better.

CHAPTER 17

STEP 2: RISK CATEGORIZATION AND SCHEDULING

Risk categorization tells us which risks we need to focus on and for how long. It also tells us which risks we can reasonably put aside, which risks can be managed by the team itself, which risk mitigations will require support and action from the project sponsor, and which ones are simply beyond the control of the project. It should be obvious that the risks we *really* want to be paying attention to are the ones that:

1. Have the highest potential negative impact on the project
2. Are the most likely to occur.

Impact and probability assessments are common tools in any PM toolbox; most PMs divide risks into "high impact" or "low impact" and "high probability" or "low probability" categories. What's much less common is a clearly understood and well-communicated idea of exactly what "high" and "low" mean for the project in question.

Beyond developing clear definitions for both impact and probability, the PM needs to understand the subtleties and strategies involved in managing risks that aren't necessarily high impact and high probability. What do we do about high-impact but low-probability risks? What about high-probability but low-impact risks?

There are six sub-steps in effective risk categorization and scheduling:

1. Defining and communicating the criteria for high- and low-impact risks

2. Adjusting the high- and low-impact criteria in light of the project priority triangle and the type of project being managed

3. Defining and communicating the criteria for high- and low-probability risks

4. Categorizing risks as red, blue, yellow, or green

5. Identifying which risks are controllable and which aren't

6. Identifying how long each risk is "alive" on the project.

Defining and Communicating Risks

If I were to ask how you'd categorize your project risks in terms of their potential impact—high or low—your answer would probably be based on two major assumptions:

1. Whether you think I'm asking about schedule, cost, or performance

2. Your definitions of *high* and *low* within these three project control elements.

Agreement on these risk assumptions must be shared and communicated with your team and your sponsor. I do this with an impact/probability grid based on a 2x2 frame that is labelled "high impact" and "low impact" along one axis and "high prob-ability" and "low probability" along the other (see Figure 17.1).

Some teams opt for more granularity, using a 3x3 grid showing high, low, and medium categories for impact and probability, but I've never found that the additional precision adds value to the exercise, so the examples in this chapter are fairly straight-forward. Risks have either a potentially high or low impact, and they either have a high likelihood (probability) of occurring or a low likelihood.

In any case, unless the criteria defining the assumptions about impact and probability are specifically outlined, it's quite pos-sible that people reading your risk grid won't have a shared understanding of the project risks. It's not enough to just cat-egorize risks in terms of high and low impact or high and low probability. It's critical that we all agree on exactly what high and low mean in terms of each of the three project control ele-ments: schedule, cost, and performance.

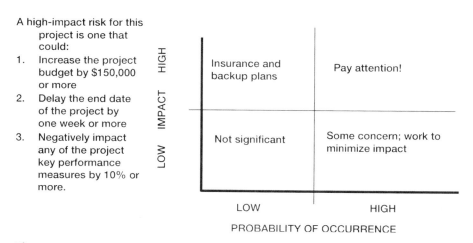

Figure 17.1 Impact/Probability Grid with High-Low-Impact Indicators

So where is the dividing line between, for example, a high-impact and a low-impact risk for cost on your project? Let's look at a project to put a new customer call center in place. The project has an estimated budget of $3 million. In this case, we will agree that any *single* risk (this is important—we're talking about the impact that any *single* occurrence of a risk turning into a risk event would have on the project) that could force an increase in budget of 5 percent or more ($150,000 or more) would fall into the high-impact category.

What about the schedule? With a projected project schedule of 40 weeks, for example, we may agree that any single risk that would delay our project—essentially a risk that would impact our critical path—by one week or more is a high-impact risk.

And performance? That's a tougher one. PMs don't usually assess risks to the performance of their projects (although they should), and that's because specific measures of project performance—objective measures that we can assess risk against—often aren't put in place. In other words, projects too often don't have "won" indicators. When good measures of performance are in place, the same disciplined risk-categorization process works when determining the impact and probability of performance risk.

Let's say that our performance targets for the call-center project are:

- A reduction of average call-handling time for customer inquiries from four minutes to under two minutes

- A reduction in call-handling staff head count by 30 percent (if we can reduce call-handling time, we won't need as many people handling calls)

- An increase in our customer satisfaction measures from 65 percent of customers reporting that they are "satisfied" or "very satisfied" to 90 percent of customers reporting that they are "satisfied" or "very satisfied" with customer service.

Now that we've established our performance targets, we can readily determine the criteria that define performance risks as high or low impact. Let's say that a reduction in one of our performance measures by 10 percent or more constitutes a high-impact risk to performance. In this case, a risk that would result in any of the following is a risk that should be categorized as high impact:

- A reduction in call-handling time by less than 81 seconds (9 seconds, or 10 percent, less than the anticipated 90-second reduction)

- A reduction in call-handling staff of 27 percent or less (3 percent less than our 30-percent target, or 10 percent of our 30-percent target)

- An increase in customer satisfaction to only 81 percent (9 percent less than our 90-percent target, or 10 percent of our 90-percent target) or less.

The PM might begin to categorize risks by asking the following questions about each risk: "If the risk we've identified became an event we'd have to deal with, could it increase our project costs by $150,000 or more? Could it push our project end date back one week or more? Could it reduce any of our three performance measures by 10 percent or more?" If the answer to *any* of the three questions is yes, the risk goes into the high-impact category, i.e., the upper half of the impact probability grid, on the *y*-axis in Figure 17.1. Using this grid ensures that team members are all aligned on what is meant by high- and low-impact risks in all three of the control elements of the project.

Adjusting Impact Criteria

Beyond your initial high-/low-impact assessment, you must consider the priorities of the project, as indicated by the project priority triangle (see Figure 17.2). If your project is time sensitive, for example, you may want to tighten up your definition of a high-impact schedule risk.

Your team may have decided that only the risks that could delay the project by a week or more should be considered high impact. With the priority triangle in mind, you might want to suggest an adjustment (see Figure 17.3):

"We met with our sponsor, and we agreed that the biggest driver on this project is the schedule. Sure, we're all concerned about the budget and project performance too, but we all agreed that our greatest sensitivity is to the end date, so I'm thinking that we might want to change the criteria for assessing high-impact risks for schedule. Maybe we should

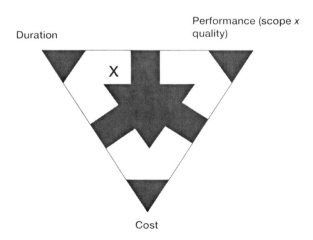

Figure 17.2 Prioritizing the Schedule

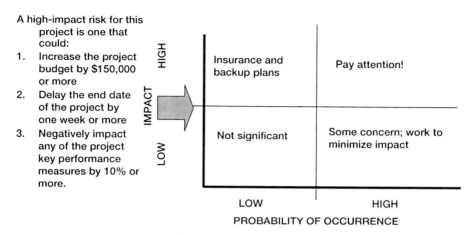

A high-impact risk for this project is one that could:

1. Increase the project budget by $150,000 or more
2. Delay the end date of the project by one week or more
3. Negatively impact any of the project key performance measures by 10% or more.

Figure 17.3 Impact/Probability Grid with High-Low-Impact Indicator

say that a risk that could affect our schedule by anything more than a day or two should be put in the high-impact category, or maybe we should agree that any risk that could have *any* negative effect on our schedule should be considered high impact."

It works the same way for cost and performance. If your project is cost sensitive—again, as indicated by the priority triangle—you may want to lower the high-impact cutoff for cost risks. If the performance measures are most significant, you may want to adjust the relevant high- and low-risk cutoff criteria. In any case, the high- and low-impact dividing line should take into consideration the additional information that the priority triangle provides.

Defining and Communicating Risk Criteria

There's a dividing line for probability on the impact/probability grid, too: the line on the *x*-axis that we'll use to divide risks that have a high and low likelihood of occurring. Probability is expressed as a percentage on the grid.

The probability dividing line illustrates a single variable—the likelihood that a given risk will occur—unlike the impact of a risk, which can affect any one, or all, of the three constraints. It's important to think about what risk probability your team is comfortable with. Experience suggests that a good high-probability marker to start with is 20 percent. If your team believes there's a 20 percent or greater chance that a risk will turn into a risk event, it's a high-probability risk, and it'll land on the right side of the grid (see Figure 17.4).

Of course, there are exceptions to the 20 percent guideline. If you're looking at risks to health and safety or the environment, for example, you may want to move the probability line back a bit. A 10 percent probability that a server won't arrive in time may rightly end up on the left of the line, in the low-probability category, but a 10 percent chance that someone will get hurt on your project surely wouldn't end up on the left—you'd adjust your probability cutoff line and put that kind of risk in the high-probability category.

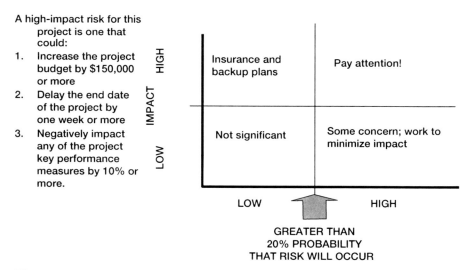

Figure 17.4 Impact/Probability Grid with High-Low-Probability Indicator

Categorizing Risks

Once you've defined the criteria for high- and low-impact/probability risks, and all participants understand the criteria, you can categorize the risks by color depending on which of the four quadrants on your impact/probability grid they fall into (see Figure 17.5):

- High-impact and high-probability risks = red risks
- High-impact and low-probability risks = yellow risks
- Low-impact and high-probability risks = blue risks
- Low-impact and low-probability risks = green risks.

Using Visuals to Illustrate Risks

I suggest building a version of the impact/probability grid on a large piece of paper or a whiteboard, then placing your risks on the grid as the team categorizes them. Use red or pink Post-it® notes to capture risks, then stick them where they belong on the impact/probability grid. Make sure that the

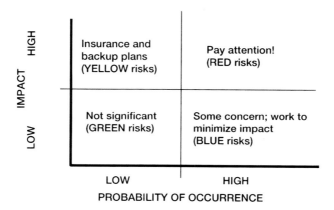

Figure 17.5 Red, Yellow, Blue, and Green Risks

criteria for high- and low-impact risks (with regard to cost, duration, and performance) and high- and low-probability risks are clearly marked on the grid.

Once the risks have been categorized as red, blue, yellow, or green, according to their position on the grid, you may want to stick the risk Post-its® on the big 3D schedule on the wall. Having the risks on the schedule itself helps the 3D reader see what kind of risks the team is facing and when each will be alive on the project.

When you move the risk Post-its® to the 3D schedule, you don't want to lose the impact/probability categorization. Office supplies to the rescue here, too—the little stick-on file flags you may be familiar with come in packages containing—you guessed it—four colors: red, blue, yellow, and green. How convenient.

Before moving the risk Post-its® to the big 3D schedule on the wall, add a colored flag to indicate the risk categorization for each one. With the indicator flags on the risk Post-its®, and the risk Post-its® on the 3D schedule, it's easy for even casual observers to see what's going on in your planning, even from across the room. Along with the 3D schedule itself, they will be able to see the risks you're dealing with, the impact and probability of those risks, and when those risks will be alive during the project.

Identifying Controllable and Uncontrollable Risks

There are some, but not many, risks you just can't do anything about, and they should be clearly identified. With enough money and time, almost every risk can be controlled or mitigated to some extent.

Keep in mind, however, that some risks just aren't worth controlling. Worried about road bans delaying access to a drilling location? You could always decide to bring the equipment you need in by helicopter and avoid the roads altogether. But that's a risk mitigation strategy that's unlikely to be accepted by management; the cost would likely far outweigh the benefit of reducing risk to the schedule. Clearly identify risks for which:

- There's no mitigation strategy the team can identify
- The incremental cost (in lengthened duration and/or increased costs and/or compromised performance) of putting a risk mitigation in place isn't deemed worthwhile.

On each risk Post-it® note, you'll want to write a C, for risks that are controllable, or a U, for those that are uncontrollable or uneconomical to control (see Figure 17.6).

In Figure 17.6, all of the C (controllable) risks here can be controlled/mitigated with some degree of intervention (for example, by air-freighting a development server in, hiring backups for accounting SMEs, or setting up a dedicated development and testing server for this project). The question is "How much is the organization willing to spend to mitigate the risk?"

The U (uncontrollable) risk is beyond the influence of the project team and cannot be easily mitigated.

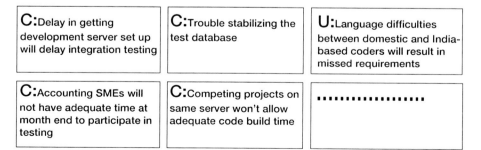

Figure 17.6 Controllable and Uncontrollable Risks

Uncontrollable risks should be brought to the attention of management, especially if they're high impact, high probability, or both, and noted explicitly in the project plan. It may be perfectly acceptable to all project stakeholders to proceed with the project if there are uncontrollable risks or risks for which risk mitigations are undesirable, but this acceptance needs to be explicit, public, and well understood.

Identifying the Lifespan of Each Risk

Just as your project has a limited life, so do the risks that will affect it. Some risks have the potential to turn into risk events at anytime during the life of the project, and some only have that potential during specific phases of the project.

The risk of losing a key resource (maybe your key subject matter expert), or the risk of a significant downturn in the price of whatever your project is producing (maybe a big decline in the price of gold during a gold mining project), may be risks that you need to be monitoring throughout the life of a project.

Other risks have limited lives; they can potentially affect the project only during a specific period of time. The risk that your development team will be competing for scarce build time on a shared development server, for example, is only alive during the development phase of your project. It doesn't exist before the team starts to write code, and it stops being a risk once it is out of development and testing.

For project risks with a limited lifespan, the lifespan should affect how and when you mitigate them. It may make sense to lease a separate development server for your team during development and testing, but it probably doesn't make sense to lease a separate box during analysis or once you're into rollout.

C: Delay in getting development server set up will delay integration testing

M4->M6

Figure 17.7 Identifying a Risk Lifespan

If development on your project starts at milestone 4 (the end of analysis and design) and ends at milestone 6 (the beginning of rollout), the risk that competition for time on the development server will mean a delay in completing code builds is only alive from milestone 4 to milestone 6. On the risk Post-it®, you'd write down "M4->M6" to indicate the risk's lifespan (see Figure 17.7).

The risk depicted in Figure 17.7 is only alive between project milestones 4 and 6. Because it's associated with integration testing, it's not alive—in other words, it's not a risk—before milestone 4 or after 6, since integration only runs between M4 and M6.

Being aware of a risk's lifespan will help your team to better focus on what needs to be done to mitigate it. Also, when evaluating progress against plan, teams should consider the period during which risks are alive. If a team reports that it is behind schedule and over budget before it even gets to a big risk window in the project—a period during which one or more big risks is alive—that may tell management that a major rethink of the project is required. It may even make sense to cancel a project under such circumstances.

On the other hand, if the team is only slightly behind schedule, slightly over budget, or both, but the big risks on the project are past the point in time during which they could have resulted in risk events, management may be much less concerned.

Once the risk categorization and scheduling work is done, you'll have information on every risk you identified:

- Its potential impact
- The probability that it'll occur
- Whether it can be controlled/mitigated or not
- The period of time during which it'll be alive.

CHAPTER 18

STEP 3: RISK MITIGATION

So what are we going to do to mitigate the risks we've identified, and what will those mitigations mean to our planning? There are eight substeps in effective risk mitigation:

1. Assessing the price of risk mitigation
2. Documenting what you've done and what you're going to do to mitigate risk
3. Managing the red risks
4. Managing the yellow risks
5. Managing the blue risks
6. Managing the green risks
7. Going after the risks that have the highest potential negative impact on the priority control element
8. Trying to avoid mitigation strategies that work against the priority control element.

Assessing the Price of Risk Mitigation

Thinking about putting extra people on the team during crunch periods on the project? What would that do to the schedule? How much would that cost? Thinking about keeping a backup drilling rig on call at all times? How much would that cost? What do each of the risk mitigations mean to the project in terms of project cost, duration, and performance?

Rule one of risk mitigation: It's never free. Risk mitigation strategies almost always involve additional deliverables, and they very often mean additional costs. One thing you most definitely don't want to do is send the signal that risk mitigation is free and that it doesn't involve any additional work. If your risk mitigation strategies appear to be free (and therefore easy), management won't make one of the most fundamental connections we need them to make on a project: Everything you do on a project has some kind of cost—a schedule cost, a financial cost, or both.

Dedicated development servers cost money; waiting for road bans to clear (mitigating the risk by waiting until after the muddy spring thaw to move equipment) adds time to the schedule. Making the cost of risk mitigations clear is consistent with the PM's mantra: Nothing in a project comes for free.

Make sure that the impacts of the risk mitigations you choose stand out on your 3D schedule. I write "RM" in easy-to-read letters in the top-right corner of the Post-its® that represent risk mitigation deliverables (see Figure 18.1). The project team

Figure 18.1 A Risk Mitigation Deliverable

and anyone else looking at the schedule can see that these deliverables are there to specifically mitigate risk, and they'll also be able to see that these mitigation deliverables, like all other deliverables on the project, will have an effort and a cost associated with them.

Assigning Risk Intelligently

Here's a really bad idea: passing risk on to another party on your project—a vendor or subcontractor, for example—just because your legal people think it's a good thing to do in general or because "we've always done it that way." Go ahead—insist that your software vendor provide all the customizations you anticipate at a fixed price, even if you're not absolutely certain how many customizations are required or how complex they'll be. Unreasonable? Yes. Expensive? Very. Unusual? Unfortunately, not very. It happens all the time.

An organization doing a project doesn't want to take any more risk on board than is absolutely necessary, so it decides the best thing to do is pass that risk on to the vendor, usually by insisting on a fixed-price agreement, even if the implications of passing on those risks aren't really clear. Besides, the contractor's lawyers—whose job, after all, is to protect their client's corporate assets—are telling them to fix-price everything they can. But a fixed-price agreement won't help the contractor at all when the vendor's money runs out, and no vendor is going to voluntarily put itself out of business for a project, no matter what the contract says.

When you come right down to it, there are really only two circumstances under which a vendor or subcontractor would accept a fixed-price arrangement, given uncertainty:

1. They're foolish, and they're "buying" the work on the basis of an optimistic estimate. Result? Watch for a brutally

restrictive change-control response from the vendor. Under a fixed-price agreement, they'll flag any change, and you'll be buried in change requests. Ever heard the line: "Bid price to win the work, change order to profitability"? As the vendor starts running beyond its original estimates, the situation will only get worse. And reminding them that they signed a fixed-price agreement won't help a bit when they declare bankruptcy.

2. They've already priced in the risk they're accepting based on uncertainty, and you'll probably never know how much you paid to pass that risk off. Because you're sticking them with all the risk of an overrun, they'll have built enough room into their fixed price that they believe they can profit despite any uncertainty. To the extent that uncertainty can be clarified, they'll make more money. And they'll still be looking for change orders.

Time-and-materials-based deals don't help much, either—they cause the opposite problem, putting most of the risk back on the client. There is, however, a middle ground: risk sharing. What if the contract target was a million dollars, with terms that benefited both parties if the project was delivered under a million and shared penalties if it went over a million? That's alignment.

Here's what I proposed on a project recently: For every dollar the project went over target, the owner would pay 50 cents on the dollar. On a million-dollar project that went to $1.2 million, the owner would pay $1.1 million—paying just 50 percent of the $200K overrun. In this case, the owner would end up paying $100K more than it had planned, and the vendor would end up doing $200K of work at 50 cents on the dollar. Thus, both parties are hurt in the case of a cost overrun, so they have a shared disincentive to go over target.

There's a second side to this arrangement too, one that encourages both parties to deliver under the target: For every dollar the project comes in under $1 million, the owner would pay the vendor 50 cents. If the project came in at $900K, the owner would write a check for $950K ($900K plus 50 percent of every dollar under a million). In this case, the vendor's margins would improve considerably—it gets a $50K bonus on $900K for going under target, and the owner runs $50K under budget. This is good for both of them; it's a shared incentive to keep costs down. Sure, there's still risk on the project, but the risk is shared, and the interests of both parties are aligned.

Putting Thoughtful Limitations on Liability

Recently, as I was reviewing a certain very big and well-known software vendor's limitation of liability clause, I saw an interesting term in a comment from outside counsel. The limitation of liability (i.e., the maximum amount for which the vendor could be sued under contract) was "aggressively limited." If this is not an oxymoron, it is a confusing concept, at least.

What the outside counsel was saying was that the owner should try, in the contract, to raise the vendor's liability for error as much as possible to cover costs that the owner might incur, even if those costs far exceed the vendor's fees. In other words, the contract may only be worth $10 million, but the damages could be $50 million, so the owner should hold the vendor accountable to that level. Good luck with that; it's only a very daring or very foolish vendor who will agree to liabilities that exceed its fees. And if it does, you'll pay for it, as an owner, somewhere else.

If a film developer loses or destroys your film, it will be liable for the value of a replacement role of raw, unexposed film, plus the cost of development. It won't pay more than that just because your pictures of your recently deceased grandma are priceless and can't be replaced. Similarly, a vendor will try to actively limit its liabilities in contract, often, conveniently, you'll note, to a maximum of the value of its errors and omissions (E&O) insurance coverage. Professional services firms, for example, often carry $2 million in E&O coverage, usually because that's what owners require they have to come on to a work site. Even on a potential $10 million contract, the vendor will try to limit its liability to the maximum of E&O.

With the owner pressing for more liability, and the vendor for less, can the parties reach a reasonable compromise? In my experience, the liability should equal the total value of fees under the agreement—no more, no less. It's reasonable that the vendor would risk up to its total fees if it makes an error, but it's unreasonable for an owner to ask for more than the value of what it has shelled out. Capping liability to equal total fees is probably an ideal compromise. Neither party will be completely happy, but that's probably just the sweet spot you want to be in.

Deciding Whether to Pass a Risk Off

Blindly passing risk off to a counterparty when there's uncertainty in the project (isn't there always?) is an amateur's error. Back in my school days, I looked at the terms on a tender document for the caissons and foundations for a big construction project on campus. The tender was pretty straightforward, except for the clauses added the end. I'm paraphrasing here, but they read something like:

> "We the owner will provide you the vendor with construction site core samples and any geotechnical studies we have on hand and for the site, but [and here's the kicker] we the owner

won't be liable for any cost overruns associated with unanticipated conditions on the site encountered during excavation."

The "unanticipated conditions" here refer to natural features
such as big boulders that would have to be removed or under-
ground water sources that would have to be dealt with during
excavation. In either event, costs could increase substantially.
So I asked the owner's representative about it.

Me: "These terms here—do you put them in every contract?"

Owner: "Yeah, our legal guys require that we put them in every
time to limit our risk of cost overruns."

Me: "I see... so how much is this risk worth to you? If you took
that clause out and took the risk on board as the owner, how
much do you think it would cost you in the end?"

Owner: "Not that much; we've built a dozen buildings on the
campus over the last few years, and we've never had a problem
with excavations. If I had to put a price on the risk, I'd say that
if we took it on board, it might cost us a quarter million."

And then I met with reps from the five companies that were
asked to bid on the tender. A typical conversation:

Me: "Did you see all those clauses associated with this tender?
What did they mean to your bid?"

Company rep: "We certainly did, and it means that if the
owner wants us to take that risk on board, it's going to cost
them money."

Me: "How much?"

Company rep: "We don't know the subsurface conditions
there very well. Even with the geotechnical study and some
samples, if they're asking us to assume that risk, it's going to
bump our bid price by a million bucks... that's a big risk for
us to take on."

The story was the same with all of the bidders. The risk premium they wanted to take on the risk was somewhere between $750K and $1.3 million—far more than it would cost the owner to assume the risk.

I think that the smart thing to do in a case like this is sit down and talk about each risk in advance of setting contract terms, then figure out which party should take on each risk, with the aim of reducing the overall project cost.

Documenting Risk Mitigation Strategies

Whatever steps you take to mitigate risk, those mitigations need to be documented in your plan. You'll need to create a risk register containing all of the information about the risks you've identified and what you're going to do about them. Begin by identifying your risk assessment criteria—the parameters your team used to assess high versus. low impact (schedule, budget, and performance) and probability. Beyond that, there should be an entry for every single risk you identify, including:

- A detailed description of the risk
- The impact of the risk
- Probability of the risk occurring
- Whether the risk is controllable or not
- When the risk is alive
- Mitigation strategy (or strategies) for that risk, including a detailed description for each mitigation
- What each mitigation is expected to do to the schedule (revised three-point estimates, otherwise known as PLOs: perfect, likely, and outrageous)
- What each mitigation is expected to do to the budget

- What each mitigation is expected to do to project performance
- Comments.

You'll also want to add columns for what *actually* happened and update the risk register as the risk window passes by:

- Did the risk actually occur?
- If it did, what was its effect on the budget, schedule, and performance?
- Did the risk mitigation appear to help avoid or mitigate the risk?

These last three pieces of information will be critical to the risk section of your project closeout report.

The risk register:

- Will be the source of information for the risk schedule that'll turn up on your status reports (see the section on risk reporting in Chapter 19 for a discussion of the risk schedule)

- Is the visible manifestation of your risk management plan, so it needs to be completed and approved *before* you can publish the baseline project plan. In fact, you can't finish your baseline planning until you've completed the first three steps of risk management:

  1. Risk identification

  2. Risk categorization and scheduling

  3. Risk mitigation.

- Will yield all of the information you need for the risk section of the closeout report.

It's important to keep both a before/without risk mitigation (WORM) schedule and budget as well as an after risk mitigation (ARM) schedule and budget.

The "before" version will reflect the budget and potential range of schedule outcomes without any specific investment in risk mitigation. The three-point estimates within will probably reflect a fairly wide (and possibly scary) range tending toward the outrageous. These will likely yield longer and more uncertain schedule estimates and probably bigger budgets—after all, if you don't invest in risk mitigations (*invest* being the key word here), you can reasonably expect your outcomes—schedule and budget—to be less certain, and you'll want more of both to cover the impact of the unmitigated risks.

The "after" versions of the schedule and budget, on the other hand, will include the additional deliverables that your mitigations require, along with a (probably) larger budget that reflects the cost of the additional risk mitigation deliverables.

Here's what I told a (frustrating) management team about the schedule and budget for a big drilling program a few years back:

We ran the first set of numbers on the project, and here's what we came up with: a 60-week schedule and about a $17 million budget. That 60 weeks reflects what we think is about a 70 percent chance of hitting the target schedule based on a Monte Carlo simulation over the range of possibilities for each phase.

But we all know that the project schedule is a priority— you've indicated that with the priority triangle—and that any production we can bring online quickly is worth a lot of money. So we took a look at what we could do to mitigate schedule risk, to tighten down the schedule ranges by investing—note the word *investing*—and we came up with a 70 percent chance of hitting a 44-week schedule with a $4 million risk mitigation strategy.

That $4 million covers bringing a couple of more rigs onto the project and building our own road in one key area to get around some weather worries—and that'll push the price of the project up to about $21 million. Given what that additional production is worth, we think it's a good investment, and that's what we'd propose.

The senior manager replied, "I have to say that I like the 44-week schedule to bring the production on line faster, but I'm not crazy about the $21 million budget. How about we aim high? How about we push a little harder and aim for the 44 weeks, but hold budget at the original $17 million?"

Me (holding my temper but also holding my ground): "I'd like to say it could work that way, but it won't. If we don't invest in the risk mitigations, our chance of hitting the 44-week schedule is just about zero. We'd be counting on none of the risks we've identified occurring, and we'd need perfect weather all year and a whole bunch of good luck on top of that.

"Risk mitigation ain't free, and it's a trade-off. We can mitigate the schedule risks and push the budget up by $4 million, or we can ignore the risks and push the schedule out by 16 weeks— one or the other. More production faster for more money or less money and production later—your choice."

No, I didn't make friends that day, but I did close the deal. And in the end, we made the 44-week schedule for just under $21 million.

My point, in case you missed it: PMs who deliver on schedule and within budget without establishing explicit and offsetting trade-offs don't do themselves or the project team any good, and worse yet, set a really bad precedent for management thinking. Their behavior gives management permission to believe that it should never accept the first schedule and budget PMs propose—"just push back every time, and you'll get a better schedule and budget."

The PM to Kill Off In Your Organization: The Wannabe Hero

I'm sure you've *never* seen this in your organization: A PM and their project team carefully lay out a schedule and budget—reflective of risk and uncertainty, of course—and the PM schedules a meeting with management to review and approve the plan. The budget? $2.5 million. The schedule? 40 weeks.

The problem, of course, is that this PM is a young up-and-comer in the organization, a "fair-haired" child thought to have loads of potential but, unfortunately, not a lot of project experience under his belt. And when said fair-haired child gets up on his hind legs in front of management with the numbers, trouble starts. Management says: "We have a lot of confidence in you, and we think you've got a bright future in this organization. We also think that with your drive and enthusiasm, you can bring this thing in for a million and a half in six months." And what does our young up and comer, full of confidence from the management stroking, say? "Will do!"

Watch out for these PMs, and when you find one, for the sake of your organization, your project, and your sanity, take them out behind the proverbial woodshed and beat them about the head with a copy of the *PMBOK® Guide*.

Managing the Red Risks

High-impact, high-probability risks are obviously the ones we need to pay the most attention to. You should expect to put in place, and a project-educated management team should expect to see, a mitigation plan for *each* of the controllable risks in this quadrant. In fact, some savvy organizations won't fund projects *at all* unless they see evidence that their project teams are putting mitigation plans in place for all the red risks they can.

Managing the Yellow Risks

If a high-impact, low-probability risk becomes a risk event, it would be very bad for the project's schedule, budget, or both, but it isn't likely to happen. Yellow risks can be thought of as "hole-in-one" risks. Let's say you're hosting a golf tournament for players like me and planning to give a new car to anyone who gets a hole-in-one. You've got yourself a high-impact, low-probability yellow risk. Fortunately, it is possible to insure against yellow risks, which is often a very effective mitigation strategy.

I visited a cogen (eration) project under construction a few years ago. Cogens burn natural gas to produce steam that is used for a heat- or steam-intensive process and that turns turbines for power generation (hence the term *cogen*). The PM on the project told me about how the team had mitigated a yellow risk on a similar project a few years before.

The critical pieces of equipment for cogens are the turbines, which are big, expensive, very sensitive, and in high demand (back-ordered 18 months). When a turbine doesn't go in on schedule, a cogen project can back up for months and cause budget overruns of tens of millions of dollars. Bottom line: Don't screw up the turbines. But screw up they did: When unloading a turbine from a rail car, the project team dropped it. Tens of thousands of pounds of drop. Turbines don't like to be dropped. Destroying a turbine? A high-impact but low-probability risk.

Fortunately, the PM's team had purchased an insurance policy before the turbine shipped as part of its risk mitigation strategy. The turbine manufacturer pulled every 20th turbine it manu-factured into a reserve set up for just such an occurrence (the reserve program was a premium), so it was able to deliver a new turbine in just weeks. The weeks of delay in getting a new tur-bine from the reserve were problematic for the project team, but the delay was not the disaster it would have been if the team had had to go to the back of the 18-month queue. The team avoided a catastrophic impact on its schedule and budget by making a relatively modest investment in a yellow-risk mitiga-tion strategy.

Yellow-risk mitigation tends to be fairly inexpensive, espe-cially if insurance is involved. Look at yellow risks carefully, even those that are about as likely as being hit by lightning, and think about what you can do to mitigate them in a cost-effective manner.

Managing the Blue Risks

Teams tend to overlook risks that are low impact but have a high likelihood of occurring. If the potential impact is below the high-impact threshold ("We wouldn't want to see it to happen, but if it did, it'd only delay us by a couple of days"), they're tempted to put these risks aside, to treat them like green risks. But that ignores cumulative impact. The impact of a single occurrence of a risk may be low, but what if it occurs a few times? It is, after all, a high-probability risk.

For example, a team was performing a series of relatively small construction/renovation projects at a hotel in a Canadian national park. Because there is greater sensitivity to the environmental impact of projects like these in national parks, projects that are considered major may be subject to a federal environmental impact review. These reviews are thorough, but they take time. The project team looked at its "small" projects and concluded that none of them were big enough to trigger a formal review. No review, no risk of a significant delay. The environmental community in the park didn't see it that way. They said that the cumulative impact of all these small projects combined to make a major project that should be subject to a review, a process that could add at least six months to the schedule. And it did.

Managing the Green Risks

The only risks that you can legitimately ignore are those that are low impact and have a low probability of occurring because the cost and effort involved in mitigating them probably outweigh the value of mitigation, but you've got to let everyone know—especially the project sponsor—that's what you're doing. You don't want to be in a situation in which the risk does come to pass but you haven't told anyone you decided *not* to do anything about it. When your sponsor says, "What the %^&*^& happened?" you probably won't get very far by saying: "Remember how we talked about this one in the spring, and remember how we all agreed that it was a low-impact and low-probability risk? And remember how we agreed not to do anything about it? Remember?" Much better to have your strategy ("Here's the risk, here's our assessment, and here's our agreement that a mitigation strategy doesn't make sense") written down in the project charter. If the risk does occur, you'll be able to handle it with less emotion, and your strategy will be less subject to the vagaries of memory.

Running a Really Useful Project Management Office: Comparing Risks across Projects

Different teams in the same organization may see the same risk in different ways, and comparing their thinking will help everybody involved. I've seen two project teams at the same Calgary-based company, both looking to ramp up natural gas production, both working in the same corner of the province, categorize the same risk in two totally different ways. Both identified the risk of a longer-than-usual spring break-up. One team saw the risk of a long thaw (i.e., longer than the two weeks they'd put in their baseline schedule) as a low-impact, low-probability green risk. The other team, however, believed it was a red risk, with a high probability of a delay and a larger negative impact, especially on schedule.

Instead of spending its time telling the teams what they had to report and how, the PMO brought this difference to the attention of each team's PM, who then brought their teams together to develop a *shared* assessment of the risk. Together, the teams decided that the risk was yellow (high impact, low probability) based on the experience of members of both teams who'd worked in that corner of the province over the last few years. Better yet, they came up with a *joint* risk mitigation plan: strategically positioning drilling rigs across both their project areas to minimize rig travel during the break-up risk period.

Break-up did take a little longer than expected that year, but because the rigs had been positioned well, the teams were able to avoid moving equipment over public roads for the period, and in the end, stayed on budget and schedule.

Going After High-Stakes Risks

If the priority triangle says that schedule is most important, more important than the budget or performance, it makes sense that in addition to turning up your sensitivity to schedule risks, you'd also go after the risks that have the biggest impact on the schedule first.

Let's take a look at a risk I mentioned earlier: the risk that your development team could be delayed during coding and testing because they'll have to share a development server with other development teams. Your developers have had to work around other teams' needs before, and they've given you a fairly wide three-point estimate for the duration of the coding and testing work effort. Two of the PLO estimates were as follows: outrageous (O) duration is 12 weeks, double the six weeks that they gave you as the likely (L) duration. Mitigations? A dedicated development server for your team might make sense. If your team didn't have to share a server with other teams, the risk of delay (for this reason) would disappear. Could that 12-week O estimate could be reduced to something closer to the six-week L estimate?

When you talk it over with the developers, they agree that a dedicated server would bring the O down to "no more than eight weeks." So far, so good, except that dedicated development servers aren't free. Let's assume that acquiring one for your team would cost $50,000, which would have to be added to the project budget.

The question, then, is should you invest an additional $50K to eliminate the risk of your development schedule lasting 12 weeks? Would we suggest spending the $50K to take four risk weeks (the original 12-week O estimate, less the new eight-week O with a dedicated server) out of the schedule?

If the priority triangle says that the priority control element is duration—that is, the schedule is more important than either the budget or project performance—spending the $50K may make sense. If the project sponsor agrees, you'd add whatever deliverables are required to acquire a dedicated server, make sure they're put in the 3D plan with adequate lead time, and increase your planned budget by $50,000.

Avoiding Particular Mitigation Strategies

But what if the priority triangle says that the budget—doing the project as cost effectively as possible and sticking to the budget you set—is the priority? In this case, it might not make sense to spend $50K to mitigate four weeks of schedule risk. In such a situation, it's important to engage key stakeholders, especially the project sponsor, to discuss appropriate trade-offs. You'll want to remind the stakeholders of the risks your team sees, talk about what you plan to do to mitigate them, and most important, discuss the costs (time and financial) that the project risk mitigation strategy entails. Sharing this information with your project sponsor will help ensure that when you're presenting the plan to management, the sponsor's got your back.

Also Keep in Mind...

- *Some mitigation strategies may positively affect more than one phase of the project.* Mitigating one risk early in a project may produce a positive effect further along. Appointing a Data Base Administrator devoted exclusively to your project, for example, may narrow your PLO estimates for a number of project phases. When you're finished mitigating risks individually, look at your risk mitigation plan holistically and consider your costs and schedule in light of the entire risk mitigation plan.

- **Risk can't be eliminated, only transferred.** Risk never disappears entirely; it just goes somewhere else. Buying insurance against an accident doesn't mean that the risk of having an accident goes away. It just means that the cost risk associated with an accident has been passed to the insurer in return for the insurance premium. Keep in mind that every risk goes somewhere, and always think about where that risk is going (see the section on assigning risk intelligently earlier in this chapter).

- **The positive impact of a risk mitigation may be less than its cost.** This should be obvious, but I've seen teams in a rush to mitigate every risk they can, proposing to spend time and money on risk mitigations that just don't make sense. This approach is like squashing a bug with a steamroller. Step back from your risk mitigation strategies at some point, and make sure that what you're proposing makes sense in light of what it would cost if the risk became a risk event. Some risks should be left unmitigated, especially those that won't have a significant impact on the project or are highly unlikely (your yellow and blue risks).

The Opposite of Risk: What about Opportunities?

Opportunities are the flip side of risk. As project teams get better at managing risk—in other words, making sure the Os in their PLOs don't happen—they start to look at what they could do to make the perfect estimates come to pass. They'll start to ask, "If we were able to achieve the P at least once in the past, what circumstances led to that P? Is there anything we can do that could make it happen again?" It may be that by eliminating a step somewhere along the line, adding resources, reducing the number of partners involved, or decreasing complexity, your team can achieve milestones closer to the P end of your estimates for work effort or duration.

CHAPTER 19

STEPS 4, 5, AND 6: RISK MANAGEMENT, REPORTING, AND CLOSEOUT

Risk management is the easiest part of the risk process. Like much good practice in project management, ongoing risk management is mostly a matter of carefully tracking performance against the baseline plan and making adjustments to that plan as things change. (Remember, "plan to manage and manage to the plan.") If new risks—that is, risks that weren't anticipated, assessed, or mitigated when the baseline plan was set—arise, they need to be added to the risk register and the risk schedule, too, along with their mitigations and the associated deliverables and costs.

These new risks and their mitigations are a little different, though. The new deliverables and their impact on schedule, budget, or both require a revision of the baseline plan, which will require you to clear the revisions with your project sponsor. You'll follow the same process if a risk event occurs that no one anticipated, although the discussion about modifying the baseline in this event will probably be a little less pleasant.

Just as there is a baseline for a project's schedule, its cost, and its expected performance, there's a baseline for its risks as well.

The risk baseline is made up of the risks the team anticipated, the risk mitigation strategies it put in place in response, and the deliverables these mitigation strategies entail. The team can create a risk schedule by adding the time periods during which the risks will be alive to a GPS (global positioning system) project tracker (see Chapter 23 for more on tracking projects with a GPS). Adding a risk schedule offers the reader of the GPS context by showing how and when the risks line up against project progress, making it a richer reporting tool and helping the reader assess overall status at each milestone. The reader can determine whether the project has passed the biggest risk window or the greatest risks are still ahead.

If you've identified a large number of risks on a project, you may, in the interest of brevity and space, decide to show only the high-impact/high-probability risks on the GPS; they're certainly the ones that readers will be want to keep their eyes on (see Figure 19.1).

There are a couple of circumstances under which risk reporting should go beyond simply showing the risk schedule:

1. *If new, unanticipated risks arise.* New risks won't be in the original project plan (although they should be added, as noted above), so they won't appear on the baseline GPS. If a new risk is added, the PM should bring it to the attention of the GPS reader by making it stand out visually on the GPS report.

2. *If a risk arises earlier or later or extends further than originally expected.* Changes to the baseline like these also should be highlighted for the reader.

Any new GPS elements requiring attention should be made to stand out with circles, stars, highlights—whatever draws attention to the fact that there's been a change since the last report that the reader should be aware of (see Figure 19.2).

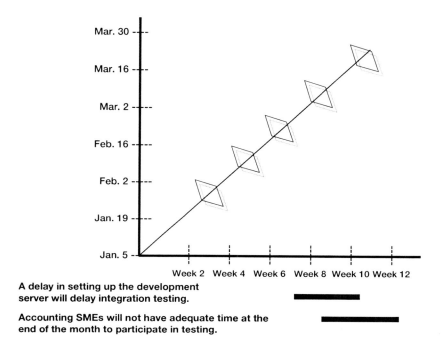

Figure 19.1 Mapping High-Impact Risks against a Schedule Baseline

Mitigations Mean Deliverables

Don't forget that a new risk means more than an addition to the GPS. It will also involve one or more new risk mitigation deliverables if a mitigation strategy for the risk is put in place. And a new deliverable or deliverables for the project will almost certainly involve a change request; deliverables don't come for free, and any additional deliverables, for risk mitigation or otherwise, must be reviewed, approved, and incorporated into a revised baseline.

The critical to-dos when closing out risks are ensuring that what's been learned is captured for the future in the project closeout report and documenting the project's risk information

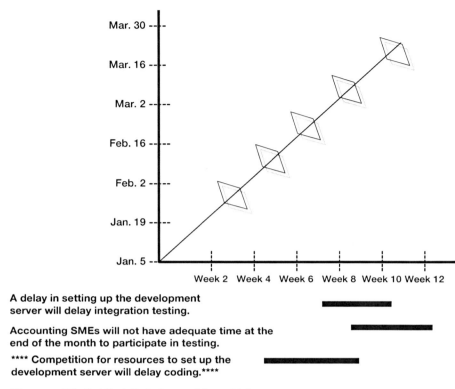

Figure 19.2 Highlighting a New Risk

in a place and a format that will be accessible to other project teams in the future. Just as the *first* deliverable of any project team should be the review of previous closeout reports, the *last* deliverable should be the creation of a closeout report for the benefit of future project teams.

At a minimum, the risk section of the closeout report should include answers to these questions:

- What risks did the project team anticipate?
- How did the project team categorize these risks in terms of their impact and probability?

- What risks did the team decide to mitigate, and what were the schedule, cost, and performance implications of those mitigations?

All of this information should, of course, be available in the baseline project plan.

The risk section of the report should also answer these questions:

- Did the mitigations work?
- What happened that the team *didn't* anticipate? What unexpected risks turned into risk events, and what were the effects of those unanticipated events on the project?
- Is there any other risk mitigation advice the team would add?

With this part of the closeout report in hand, future project teams will benefit from the experience of those that came before. This doesn't happen nearly often enough today.

One more good reason to mandate a risk section in the project closeout report: If a team knows that its risk planning (and its success or failure) will live on in posterity, it'll probably look at the risks in its project a little more carefully in the first place.

CHAPTER 20

SETTING CHECKPOINTS AND OFF-RAMPS

It's absolutely necessary to set the (objective, readily measurable) conditions of success for your project (the "wons") *before* you even finish planning it so that your planning can incorporate everything that will be needed to achieve these expectations. You must have a clear view of the end of your project before you start, but this still isn't enough. Beyond determining your "wons," you have to decide *how* you're going to know whether your project is succeeding as you go.

One of the first questions I ask PMs when I'm reviewing their ongoing projects is, "How is your project going?" If the project isn't in (visible) distress, I usually get some variation of "good," "fine," or "we're OK." It's the next question that throws 'em off: "How do you know?" Even if I'm not there to ask you this question, you'd better believe your stakeholder community, and especially your sponsor, is wondering, even if they don't say it out loud.

The PMs often hesitate when I ask this. To clarify, I'll say, "What I mean is, what are you seeing right now on your project that tells you you're being successful? What's telling you that you're heading to a successful conclusion?" I don't always get a blank stare in response. Sometimes I get: "Well, we're on schedule and on budget." As I've said before, neither of those are particularly strong indicators of a successful project.

Stronger signs of success come from not only defining in advance what a successful project will look like at the end but, also, establishing markers that will tell you how successful you are while the project is in progress. If you don't set explicit interim performance markers, called *checkpoints*, in your plan and schedule, you and everyone else are left to guess how well an ongoing project is going. If you don't have checkpoints, the only way to do this is to sort through the often-inadequate technical project reporting information teams usually produce. This reporting is mostly:

- Based on cost and schedule, neither of which say anything about the performance of the project
- Backward looking, telling us what's happened in the past, but offering very little forecasting (see Chapter 22 for more about effective reporting).

Checkpoints (and the big brother of the checkpoint, the *off-ramp*) are the answer. If you say that your project is "going very well, thank you for asking," and someone like me follows up with "How do you know?" you'll be able to say, "Let me *show* you how we know. We set checkpoints, with objective measures, at the beginning of the project, including the dates we expected to see those objective measures arise, and we're actively tracking against them."

Checkpoints and off-ramps are laid on top of the 3D schedule you prepared and are represented by major business-oriented deliverables. As a general rule, checkpoints and off-ramps are always set at a milestone, but not every milestone will have a checkpoint or off-ramp.

Checkpoints are represented by stories that tell you what conditions you should expect to see at each point. These stories are much more than just a recitation of deliverables for each checkpoint. "We know we're on track because we delivered all the deliverables we expected to at the most recent project milestone" isn't enough. It *is* good news that "the survey database server was installed on schedule" and "the data extract was completed and exported on schedule," but these aren't the kind of business-oriented, stakeholder-aware deliverables that will give your stakeholder community a warm feeling about project progress. The president of your company may care, at some level, about the server and the database, and you may see these deliverables as a proxy for progress, but they don't really mean much in the language the president would understand.

If the president could articulate what he's looking for, he'd probably say, "Technical stuff aside, what have you got that shows me that progress is being made against the end-of-project measures of success you made me sign off on at the beginning of this project? What have you got, in terms that mean something to me, that relates to the ultimate success of this project?"

Let's say that ultimate success for a project (the answer to "How do we know we've won?") is defined as follows:

Within six months of going live with the new customer call-center support system:

- We've reduced average call-handling time from more than four minutes to less than two minutes
- We've reduced the number of staff in our call-handling center by 30 percent
- We've increased our average measure of customer satisfaction, as measured on a 100 percent scale, from 60 percent on average to more than 85 percent on average.

This is a good, solid set of measures, each with a distinct, objective deliverable for the project team to aim for.

The interim measures of success—the deliverables that make up a business story that indicates progress toward success have to be just as objective, and they must have a strong link that the president would appreciate to the ultimate "won" measures. If you say, "Our interim measure of success is that the server is up," the President might say, "What does that have to do with reducing our average call time and increasing our customer satisfaction?" A better, more directly relevant measure of success might be running an interim test in three pilot states.

If your project has no real business-oriented measures of success as you move along, if you really won't have any idea if you've achieved what you set out to do until the very end, best to let the stakeholder community know that at the beginning, too. It just may be that there *aren't* any interim measures of success for your project, that aside from the technical project reporting (traditional deliverables, budgets and schedules, and their forecasts), you *won't* know until it's done. A lack of interim business-oriented markers of progress is OK, as long as the entire stakeholder community understands and agrees to that in advance.

Off-Ramps: The Big Brother of the Checkpoint

Robert De Niro has a great line relevant for PMs in the movie *Ronin*. Going to meet a bunch of questionable criminals-for-hire in a shabby bar in Paris, he hedges his bets by hiding a gun under a milk crate at the back door before he enters the bar. When the leader of this group of criminals-for-hire sees what he's done, she confronts De Niro's character: "I saw what you did with the gun at the back door—what's that all about?" De Niro gives the perfect PM's answer: "Lady, I never walk into a room without a plan for walking back out again."

Do you have a plan for "walking back out again?" What will you do if your project gets so off-track that it should be cancelled? Have you planned for cancellation? More important, have you identified the conditions in advance that will tell you it makes sense to cancel the project, certainly ahead of anyone else telling you it should be cancelled?

Good PMs aren't surprised when bad projects are cancelled; they identify the conditions in advance (just like they do for checkpoints) that tell them they should be stopping, and with the support of a good sponsor, they do.

Must-Do Projects

There's really no such thing as a must-do project, regulatory requirements, executive speeches, and edicts aside. I've asked clients whether their must-do projects would still be essential if the projects' budgets and schedules both doubled (not that we've ever seen that happen before). The answer is usually, "Well, under those kind of circumstances, it might not really be must do." Even under threat of fine and sanction, projects can go so off the rail that it makes sense to cancel them and incur penalties rather than finish them. Every PM needs to answer this question in advance: Under what circumstances would it make sense to cancel this project, and should we put appropriate cancellation plans in place?

Don't Cancel Too Late

There's no crime in cancelling a project under two conditions:

1. You've identified, in advance, the conditions under which it makes sense to cancel and agreed to them with your sponsor

2. You're cancelling early enough for resources to be reallocated effectively.

PART 3

MANAGING TO THE PLAN

Managing a project is easy; it's a logical by-product of a solid plan. The next few chapters of this book are all about managing to the plan you've made. And if you're not managing to the plan you've made, if it's just a series of documents gathering dust on a shelf, what *are* you managing?

CHAPTER 21

CHANGE IMPACT MANAGEMENT: CHANGE IS NEVER FREE

The art of progress is to preserve order amid change and to preserve change amid order.

—Alfred North Whitehead

Effective change impact management is the calling card of competent project managers, though it represents only the *minimal* standard of competence for PMs. Aside from the many other competencies they need to embody, this one is foundational. To paraphrase Gene Kelly's character in *An American in Paris*, if you can't manage project changes effectively, give it up and marry the boss's daughter. Managing change as a project progresses really isn't that hard to do if you have three things solidly in place:

1. Discipline in assessing change
2. Consistency in responding to it
3. A project baseline that can be used to determine and communicate the impact of change.

Let's start our discussion of discipline with a few words on terminology. *Change control*, aside from being one of those terms that make project managers sound like bureaucrats (*project management office* is another), has always been something of a misnomer. Can you really *control* change on a project?

Avoiding the term *change control*, then, we're left with the marginally better but often confusing term *change management* (which has all sorts of implications beyond project management itself), or better yet, *change impact management*. If it's done well, change impact management involves the disciplined identification, assessment, and management of *all* changes, either potential (*change requests*) or approved (*change orders*), that could have an *impact* on a project's performance, budget, or schedule. (Every *italicized* word in this paragraph is italicized for a very good reason.)

Calling the process *change impact management* is consistent with a PM best practice: using clear, descriptive, and results-based project names. *Change impact management* is clear. *Change control* isn't.

More terminology: There's an important difference between a *change request* and a *change order*. It's a change request *before* it's been approved; it's a change order only *after* it's been approved and the cost, duration, and performance impacts have been communicated and signed off. After the analysis of the impact of a potential change (in terms of schedule, budget, and performance) is completed, a change request is prepared, and it continues to be a change request until it's explicitly approved— until the approver (usually the project sponsor) agrees that the changes are important enough to compensate for their effects on schedule, budget, or performance and that the project baseline will be revised accordingly.

Projects of any significant size will have pending change requests, those that are waiting to be approved and turned into change orders; rejected change requests, those that the sponsor,

---

Dr. No: Now *There's* an Effective Project Sponsor

I recently worked with a sponsor who was proud to refer to himself as Dr. No. To keep the project rolling on, he was happy to reject a lot of changes—most, in fact—that other project stakeholders thought they needed. To his credit, he never let the PM take the heat for his saying no. If a stakeholder had a problem with the sponsor's decision, the sponsor (bless him) believed that it was *his* role to communicate his thinking on the question. Because he was accountable for the success of the project—as any good sponsor should be—he was also directly and visibly accountable for decisions regarding changes to the project baseline he'd signed off on.

---

like Dr. No, won't agree to; and approved change orders, which are reflected in a revised project baseline.

Keep in mind that any or all project change requests may not be accepted. The hit to the schedule, budget, or performance that will result from the change might just be too much for the hosting organization to accept. Only after formal approval does a change request become a change order, and only then can the PM and team act on it. And the first thing to do, post-change-request approval, is to adjust the project baseline to reflect the impact of the change order on budget, schedule, or performance, giving us a revised baseline.

Defining Change Impact Management

Any material change in the project environment (and more changes are material than you might think) has an impact on project schedule, budget, or performance. Pretending that they won't have an effect—that is, accepting a change without recognizing an impact on schedule, budget, or performance—sends a message, directly or not, that your project is carrying slack, that somewhere in your plan you have spare cycles or spare dollars or spare something that'll allow you to "suck it up" without an impact. That's a bad message to send. And you're certain to lose the levers of change control if you do. Let a change slip by once without any impact, and people will expect to make other changes without impacts too—a dangerous precedent. Ignoring the impact of changes leads to the negative assumptions people make about contingency.

Why Contingency Is a Bad Idea

Talking to a client about how his organization could tighten up its project governance and management practices, I suggested that one of the first things it could do was "get rid of the contingencies you guys put in every project budget." He was skeptical about the suggestion. "Why would we want to do that?" he asked. "We blow through too many of our project budgets as it is now. If we didn't have contingencies, it would be even worse."

"So how many of your projects end up using their contingency?" I pressed.

He thought a minute: "I guess I can't think of any that haven't, ultimately, used it."

I didn't have to say it: If contingency is used every time, doesn't it stop being *contingency*? Isn't it, in the end, just another part of the baseline budget, with another name?

Setting a contingency amount for projects and using it every time is just like installing a door but never closing that door: It's pointless. Beyond that, contingency tends to be terribly abused. When people know that a project has contingency, they'll reach for it to cover the sin of every delay. When a project has contingency, you may hear this kind of conversation:

> PM: "Are you on track for that business requirements deliverable due next Friday?"
>
> "We're a little behind," a team member replies. "I think we'll need a couple of more weeks to get it done."
>
> Not pleased with that answer, the PM might say: "But that's a key deliverable that a whole bunch of other deliverables are depending on. I think maybe you and I should sit down with the sponsor to talk the impacts of this one through."
>
> "Not necessary," the team member may say. "There's no real impact and no need to involve the sponsor; we just assumed you'd take it out of the contingency."

And that's the thing about having contingency in a project: Everybody thinks they own it, and there's a tendency to use it to cover up issues as they arise, rather than dealing with them and their impact immediately. Just as certain drugs given to racehorses tend to mask the underlying problems caused by a horse's injuries, contingency tends to mask underlying issues in a project. These issues often don't turn up until the contingency is exhausted, when it's usually too late to respond effectively.

Let's imagine the same conversation regarding a project that doesn't have contingency.

> PM: "Are you on track for that business requirements deliverable due next Friday?"
>
> "We're a little behind," a team member replies. "I think we'll need a couple of more weeks to get it done."
>
> PM: "OK, we can do that, but that'll push our end date out two weeks."
>
> Team member: "Can't we just say we'll take it out of contingency?"
>
> PM: "Nope—don't have any."
>
> That'll get the team member's attention focused on making deliverables on time.
>
> Note that it may be wise to retain some contingency within an overall budget at the program level if a single change requiring additional funding could throw an entire budget cycle into a twist.

A couple of years back, we were deep into analysis and design for an extension to the client's financial system when the CFO, one of the two sponsors, left the organization, and a new CFO/sponsor was appointed, in this case through an internal promotion from another division. The co-sponsors (in this case, the COO and the new CFO) were surprised when I put in a change request.

"What's this for?" they asked.

"The impact that getting you," I was looking at the new CFO, "up to speed and getting your approval on the decisions made to date is going to have on the schedule and cost of the project."

"How will that affect the schedule and cost?" they asked.

"You," I was looking at the CFO again," told the business analysts last week that since you were new to the project, you needed to review our analysis and design to date before you approved the configuration we're proposing. That makes sense, but it meant that you weren't in a position to meet the original sign-off dates in the plan."

"Yes, I did, but what if I don't want to make any changes?"

"Even if you don't, we'd have to back off the approval dates," I said.

"You're doing pretty well so far... can't you make it up somewhere else?"

"Not really. We don't have any slack in the schedule at all, per our agreement when the plan was signed off, and business sign-off is on the critical path. Any delay on approval means a delay further down the line."

"So you're saying you don't think I should take the time to review?"

"On the contrary, I think the review is a good idea. I can't see putting in changes that you don't agree with. It's just that we'll need to reflect the time it'll take for your review in the schedule and the budget. And we need to be prepared for other changes if you see anything in the design to date that you want to change."

Not a popular message, granted, but anything else would have been dishonest, and the team would have had to deal with the impact later, in any case. Remember, it's better to eat your crow when it's young and tender...

Managing Change in Three Dimensions

Every PM knows that if something (some product, some service) needed for a project comes in at a higher price than was originally forecasted in the baseline budget, a change request aimed at eliciting the formal approval to revise project spending and adjust or rebaseline the project budget is in order. And almost every PM knows that if something is being delivered or constructed later than in the original schedule, a schedule-based change request is in order.

What most PMs *don't* do is watch for changes that have an effect on a project's ultimate *performance*, and they don't invoke the change management process as consistently here as they do for changes in budget and schedule.

Starting from a Baseline

Based on everything we have in the plan, along with a reasoned and well-thought-out assessment of the uncertainty and risk we're dealing with, there are three components (seeing a recurring theme here?) to a project planning baseline:

- Schedule
- Budget
- Performance.

A change may have an effect on just one of the control elements, but it might affect two or all three.

If you haven't established a baseline in all three dimensions before you start dealing with change, you've got trouble—trouble in the form of people assuming that what they want isn't, in fact, a change ("Why are you giving me a change request? We always assumed that this was in the plan."). How *would* you assess and communicate change if you didn't have a baseline off which to evaluate change?

Using the Change Management Process

When was the last time you submitted a change request to *reduce* a project budget or to *shorten* a schedule? One of the reasons that management is skeptical about PMs and our processes (including change impact management) is that change requests are so often "changes up." "We're always getting asked to approve changes that mean that projects are going to cost more or that things are going to be delivered later," said one exasperated exec, "but I've never seen a request to give money back or deliver earlier. And you wonder why I'm not crazy about meetings with PMs and the whole change-order thing?"

He's right: change management should not be a vehicle to bludgeon management with every time something is added to a project. Being disciplined with change requests is a good way to build credibility. This means being as willing to give money or schedule back when you don't need it—in other words, to make a "down" change request—as you are to ask for extra time or money when you really need it.

Revising the Baseline

Changing the baseline as necessary is a matter of simple project management mechanics. Here's the rule: The end results of the project (schedule, cost, performance) will be the net of the baseline for all three plus or minus the change orders. If your project doesn't add up like that, changes got away without change orders, which is a bad thing.

PMs who keep this simple math in mind will be vigilant about, and responsive to, changes in the project environment. And no,

I don't accept the argument that this makes a project too bureaucratic. Without discipline, a project will be out of control.

Even if you're an Agile user (I'm a fan, with the caveat that using Agile is not an excuse for sloppy or less diligent project management), anything you learn from each sprint (or even if budget or schedule are adjusted within a sprint, which should never be the case in pure Agile) that will change plans for the next sprint must be reflected in a change request/order. Agile is a way of approaching system development, it isn't a different way to manage projects. Isn't each sprint in an Agile project really just a smaller project itself? Next time someone tells you that he doesn't need this project management stuff because he's doing an Agile project, cuff him across the back of the head for me, will you?

CHAPTER 22

USEFUL, RELEVANT, READABLE REPORTING

When I'm asked to comment on the effectiveness of reporting for a project in progress, to review a proposed reporting format for a project just starting up, or to comment on a "new" standardized reporting regime from yet another well-intentioned but misguided Project Management Office (yes, this can be an exciting business), I'm often presented with colorful, multipage reporting productions, complete with elegantly articulated Gantt charts and enough red, green, and yellow status indicators to light up a Christmas tree. And invariably, these celebrations of project reporting make me think of a scene from Douglas Adams' *The Hitchhiker's Guide to the Galaxy.*

In said scene, two of the main characters, Arthur Dent and Ford Prefect, are being held captive in a Volgon warship. This is a bad thing. Their miraculous escape—a good thing—is engineered through the use of something called an Infinite Improbability Drive, which, true to its name, immediately generates an almost infinitely improbable event wherein Arthur and Ford are removed from certain death at the hands of the Volgons, only to be deposited in empty space outside the Volgon warship, where death is even more imminent and even more certain than it was when they were inside.

In describing this predicament, another character, Zaphod Beeblebrox, summarizes how I feel about some of these weighty, colorful, and almost entirely useless project reports: "OK, so ten out of ten for style but minus several million for good thinking, yeah?"

My major complaint comes down to this: These reports don't tell the reader what they really want to know (or *should* really want to know) about a project because:

They put the emphasis on the wrong stuff—the tasks and activities, rather than the deliverables. Our progress should be measured and reported against the deliverables that we said we'd produce, not just the activities and tasks we're checking off.

A marketing VP I once worked for said, "What matters is what you put in my hands to use—that project stuff you do on the way to what you put in my hands? I don't give a damn." Smooth he wasn't; deliverables focused he was.

If we're doing it right, the project deliverables, some of which are directly linked to our measures of success (our "wons"), along with when we plan to deliver those deliverables, should be the foundation of our planning and, therefore, the most important stuff we track and report against. Task and activity reporting doesn't mean much to anyone beyond the project team itself.

They (sometimes) put the emphasis on dates—more of the wrong stuff. Most of the project reports I see focus on the easiest—and probably least important—thing to report on: project dates. Simply finishing a project task or activity on time can be largely irrelevant to the performance objectives of the project, and our traditional way of reporting progress against a schedule looks even weaker. This is especially true if date isn't the key driver on the project. If project performance or the project budget are even more important to the ultimate success of the project than making dates, reporting that emphasizes dates at the expense of other information is at best misdirected and at worst largely irrelevant.

They're based on lousy communication tools. Worse yet, activity and task progress is often reported via Gantt or PERT charts. Gantts and PERTs are tools that we PMs use to plan our projects, but as vehicles for communicating with our stakeholder community (most of whom are not project managers), they, well, stink, despite what you might hear others say.

They're backward looking. Most project reporting I've seen is historic. It tells us where we've been, but it doesn't tell us anything about where we're going, which is all we can really do anything about at this point.

And adding dashboard reporting to the mix only helps a little bit. It gives us the current state of the project but doesn't tell us anything about what's ahead. That's why dashboard reporting is a really dumb idea. What do the indicators on the dashboard of your car tell you? How fast you're going? How far you've come? Maybe how long you've been driving, and maybe even how much gas you've burned in getting to where you are? What a dashboard *doesn't* tell you is probably what you need to know the most: *where* you're going and *how long* it might take you to get there based on the information you have up to now. The shortcomings of a dashboard are the same ones that exist in a project report that focuses on the past: Neither provides a forecast.

While the past is interesting and may hold valuable lessons for the future, it's far more important that our reporting looks ahead, that it provides a forecast for what will happen in the future, a forecast that allows us to make changes now in order to influence future outcomes. A project GPS—global positioning system—can do that for us (see Chapter 23).

They're simplified to the point of being simplistic. And while we're on the subject of dashboards and driving, whoever said that red, green, and yellow lights are good indicators of project status? Sure, simplicity can be a good thing, but sometimes we oversimplify important or complex information.

The Hitchhiker's Guide to the Galaxy (said to be "the standard repository of all knowledge and wisdom in the Universe") contains an entry for our planet, as follows: "Earth: harmless."

A gross oversimplification, much to the consternation of earthling Arthur Dent, who lobbies for a comprehensive entry that more accurately reflects the complexity of his home planet. The next edition is updated accordingly: "Earth: mostly harmless."

Oversimplification of project reporting is an easy trap to fall into. Sometimes:

- It's easier for the project team: "I hate this reporting stuff—can't we just do the project?"
- Management just wants something simple: "Can't you just give it to us on one page?"
- More ominously, simplification allows us to gloss over a multitude of project sins: "Yeah, I know we're a little behind, but it's the learning curve—we'll catch up."

Because you shouldn't complain about bad ideas unless you've got better ideas, here are my suggestions for improved project reporting, based on four principles.

Principle 1: Plan to Manage and Manage to the Plan

Once you have a solid plan in place (and you've shared it with the entire stakeholder community), you should prepare to report progress and forecast future outcomes based on that plan. It's an amateur's error to separate planning from reporting. You've said what you intend to do and how you intend to manage in three dimensions (schedule, budget, and performance), now it's up to you to report accordingly. How you plan a project should lead naturally to how you track it and report on it. What this means is that your project reporting (and for the balance of this chapter, I'll use the word *reporting* as a proxy for the trinity of tracking, control, and reporting) should emphasize project performance if that's what your planning emphasized. On the other hand, if your priority is tight adherence to a budget, your reporting should emphasize cost tracking accordingly, and if schedule is the big issue, I'd expect schedule tracking to play the biggest role.

Assuming that all three measures are important to a greater or lesser extent, your baseline, and any reporting and forecasting against it, will incorporate all three:

1. *The schedule you expect to adhere to.* What deliverables do you expect to deliver, at which milestones, and on which dates?
2. *The budget you expect to manage by.* How much do you plan to spend overall, and how is that spending expected to add up, milestone by milestone?
3. *The performance you expect the project to achieve.* What are the interim and ultimate measures by which the success of the project will be defined, and when do you expect them to be achieved?

If you were careful to ensure that you had a clear idea of what the end of your successful project would look like before you got started, you should have a tight plan to track against. Remember that:

- "Done" anchors the project end point. It tells you and the entire stakeholder community what deliverables constitute a *finished* project (not, please note, that you've necessarily finished it to the expected level of performance), and your reporting should look forward to these important deliverables.

- "Won" represents the deliverables that will tell you (and again, everyone else) that the project has delivered the planned level of *performance*. If the "won" criteria are important to your plan, they should also be important to your reporting.

Principle 2: Make Reports Meaningful

Effective reporting means reporting on your progress toward each of the three key measures. Schedule? Pretty straightforward: Have you delivered the deliverables you said you'd deliver on the dates you said you'd deliver them, or are the deliverables early or late? Budget? Pretty straightforward, too: Are you committing the sponsoring organization to the costs you expected, or have you overspent or underspent at the reporting milestone?

Dumb Idea: Reporting on Accounting Actuals Rather than Commitments

Note that I talk about reporting on *commitments*, rather than on accounting *actuals*. Accounting systems tend to count stuff that happened in the past (usually 45 to 60 days behind where you now are) such as checks that have already been sent following the processing of invoices. Commitments don't usually come through accounting, which is why we PMs usually keep our own spreadsheets that track commitments (money that the project is obligated or has agreed or is contracted to pay), even if the work hasn't been done yet, even if invoices haven't been received, and certainly before checks have been released out of the accounting system.

A better idea? Pay attention and track what you know you're committed to on the project—accounting systems are usually too far behind to be really helpful to a PM. And that, by the way, is why it's also a dumb idea to spend big money connecting accounting systems to PM systems.

Performance? Measuring your progress toward a "won" is tough but absolutely necessary. As a starting point, ask your project team, "Can we think of any interim indicators that will tell us and all our stakeholders about how we're doing toward our ultimate performance goals?" Just because the answers don't come to mind readily doesn't mean the question should be put aside. I guarantee that if I'm reviewing your project, this is one of the two first questions I'll be asking. I'll start with, "How's it going?" If the answer I get is "It's going well," I'll then ask about interim measures: "So how do you *know* it's going well?" The question is intended to find out if the team has identified any interim indicators of successful performance.

Some project managers try to offer comfort by reporting that the project is on time and on budget, as if that really gives any indication that the project will deliver on its ultimate perform-ance objectives. Adherence to schedule and budget is good and important, but as you know, it *isn't* a proxy for interim project performance measures, and it isn't an adequate answer to the question.

And this is why project team members have to put their heads together and do the hard work of identifying interim performance indicators that will actually tell the team it's progressing apace toward its ultimate performance goals. A temptation here will be to simply report on interim deliverables, even if those deliverables don't directly correlate to project performance objectives. Resist the temptation.

I remember the technical lead for the call-center project described earlier telling me, "We'll know it's going well at milestone 3, five months in, if the server we're going to run this thing on is up and operational." An operational server is no doubt an important deliverable, but it's not the kind that's going to warm the heart of the CEO, who wants to know how the team is doing against the ultimate goal of the project, such as reducing call-handling time. The fact that a server is up on schedule, while good news in and of itself, doesn't tell the CEO anything useful about the measures he really cares about.

Here's a better interim performance indicator for the call-center project: The team had planned to pilot the new call-handling software in three U.S. states before rolling it out across the rest of the country. The team believed that if it was on the right track, average call-handling times in the three pilot states would fall to about three minutes, on the way to an average time of less than two minutes when the system was up and operating nationally and all the customer support reps had been fully trained.

With this interim measure established, the team could say to the CEO, "We'll know it's going well if, at milestone 4, we can reduce average call-handling times in the three pilot states to less than three minutes. That'll give us a good feel for the progress we're making toward our ultimate goal." That's the kind of measure of interim performance that sponsors and the stakeholder community understand. They really don't care as much about the project mechanics—adherence to the schedule and budget or technical deliverables—as they do about your progress against the way they're really going to measure success: your "wons."

Principle 3: Look Forward

You'll need to track your three key reporting elements (again, schedule, budget, and performance) in three ways to adhere to this principle:

1. *Baseline:* The basis of your plan, which must be approved by your sponsor and communicated to all stakeholders before project performance measurement can begin. The baseline is the deliverable that more or less indicates the point at which project planning ends and project execution and management begins. (As an aside, when the baseline plan is approved, the change impact management process kicks in. Any changes in schedule, budget, or performance from this point forward are subject to a disciplined change impact management process. Remember, nothing changes for free.)

2. *Actuals:* Reporting that indicates how you're doing against each of your three planning elements at each milestone in the project as you reach them. Tracking of project actuals answers three questions:

   • How are we doing at this point against our planned schedule—are we delivering the deliverables we expected to deliver at the times we expected to deliver them?

   • How are we doing at this point against our planned budget—are we spending the project budget at the pace we expected?

   • How are we doing against our interim indicators and toward our expected measures of success (our "wons")?

3. *Forecast:* Based on where we are for schedule, cost, and performance at each milestone, what do we forecast for our schedule, costs, and performance at each milestone in the future? What is what we're seeing now telling us about the future? What if we're two weeks behind schedule now—should we expect to finish at least two weeks late? If we've underspent by $100,000 at this point, but we've made all the deliverables on schedule, can we forecast ending the project below budget? Should we "give back" the $100K and reduce the overall budget accordingly?

Principle 4: Report and Track Project Deliverables in Binary Terms

Good reporting is a one-or-zero, on-or-off, deliverables-are-either-complete-or-they're-not kind of business. Good reporting doesn't depend on speculation or intuition or guesswork. Your deliverables are either complete or they're not. Give no credit for the "we're almost finished" deliverables or the "we're 99 percent done" deliverables. Reporting "almost done" is asking for trouble.

A Dumb Idea: Reporting Percentage Complete

The problems with reporting on percentage complete, especially on technology projects, are numerous. How *do* you apply a percentage complete to a deliverable if you can't readily see and touch its progress? Sure, 50 percent complete on the pour for a building foundation is, relatively speaking, easy to confirm: If 50 percent of the foundation is filled with concrete (subject to inspection, of course), it can be convincingly argued that 50 percent of the deliverable is complete, so a 50 percent completion should be reported accordingly, 50 percent of the value of the deliverable has been earned, and 50 percent of the value of the deliverable should be paid accordingly.

But what does 50 percent complete mean in requirements analysis? What objectively constitutes 50 percent of a completed design? Even tougher to measure: What does 50 percent complete on a software program look like? Applying percentages to deliverables like these and making progress payments based on them is far too subjective for my liking.

Further, percentage-complete progress on these deliverables tends to be subject to rapid progress inflation in the early stages; it then has a disconcerting habit of slowing to a crawl as the project nears completion. Ever notice that a deliverable can be reported as "90 percent complete—we're just about done" at the end of the first week, then "95 percent finished—we're almost there" at the end of the next week, followed by "98 percent done—just the cleanup left" the week after, and on to "99.5 percent finished—any minute now" the week after that?

There's an occupational risk for any PM reporting percentage-complete measurements that are subject to the judgement of the person measuring progress. And that's why I'm so hesitant to use them. A better idea? Binary reporting: recognizing that a deliverable is either done or it isn't done. No percentage complete, just finished or not finished, just 1 or 0, just yes or no. If some of your deliverables are too big to be completed within a reasonable period and reporting progress toward completion as "zero" or "not finished" doesn't accurately reflect the progress made, break them down into smaller sub-deliverables. If the sub-deliverables are of a manageable size, you can report them as completely, objectively, entirely complete or not—a much better way, I think, to report progress.

This kind of binary reporting also demands binary planning and clear and unequivocal deliverables. Too many project plans—and the reporting that follows—are based on activities that don't result in tangible deliverables.

I'm not a fan of planning for and reporting on project activities, and in my experience, neither are most sponsoring executives. They really don't care that much about the team's activities; what they *really* want to know is what the team is *producing*, what it's *delivering*, and what these deliverables have to do with the ultimate performance objectives of the project.

On a bigger project, granted, a PM probably needs to plan for and track activities at a lower level for themselves and the project team, but the sponsor and stakeholders don't likely care, for example, that the PM has a project activity such as holding a planning meeting to lay out a testing strategy. They may, on the other hand, care when the testing strategy is *delivered*. Look at these three activities:

- Activity: Hold meetings with accounting leadership team
- Activity: Interview field crew about how process flow control works
- Activity: Meet about pilot test data sets.

Note that all of these activities are expressed in the present tense. Deliverables should be expressed in the past tense if they are finished—that is, if they have been delivered. For example:

- Deliverable: Meetings with accounting leadership team *held*, and reports on what accounting expects to see for monthly, quarterly, and annual financial reporting *documented*, *reviewed*, and *delivered* to project business analyst

- Deliverable: Field crews *interviewed* and process flow control processes *documented* in Visio according to business analysis process modeling standards, *approved* by field crews, and *delivered* to project analysts

- Deliverable: Pilot test data sets *confirmed* and data requirements *delivered* to the project Data Base Administration.

Yes, these descriptions are long, but they're absolutely clear. And the deliverables are specific and binary; it's pretty easy to tell if they're finished (delivered) or not. The "-ed" endings on the deliverables' names are important—they indicate that the deliverables are complete (*reviewed*, *delivered*, *documented*) rather than in progress. Using past-tense verbs facilitates binary reporting.

By reporting on what is absolutely complete and when, we can claim the appropriate project milestones. This method of reporting also makes clear what is not complete; if a deliverable at a milestone isn't complete, our reporting should clearly and visibly show that we're late.

Chapter 23

Putting It All Together: Single-Page Reporting and the GPS

Our objective is reporting that supports the five principles discussed in Chapter 22 and meets four criteria:

1. *Objective:* Based on measures that are easy for everyone, including the PM, the project team, the sponsor, and any project stakeholder, to use to evaluate progress
2. *Deliverables based:* Focused on progress toward delivering what the team committed to deliver in the baseline plan
3. *Clear:* Graphical and easy to read, without requiring the reader to have any formal project management training
4. *Forward looking:* Forecasts where the project is going almost as well as it tells the reader where the project has been.

We can put together a straightforward reporting framework that meets these criteria, and even better, we can do it in one page (OK, maybe two pages if we feel the need to add commentary) that incorporates 11 reporting elements. Start by tracking and reporting on the three key control elements of your project:

1. Schedule
2. Cost
3. Performance.

Each of these three elements should be reported on in three dimensions: baseline, actuals, and forecast.

a. *Baseline.* According to our original, approved plan, how do we propose to show progress on schedule, costs, and performance at each milestone?

The Critical Importance of Establishing a Baseline

Any PM who starts to manage a project—and I'm drawing a clear distinction here between *planning* a project and *managing* a project based on the approved plan—*before* the baseline is set and widely agreed upon puts themselves at considerable risk. Without a clear delineation between the end of planning and the beginning of execution, or "project management," the PM's ability to manage a disciplined change impact management process is seriously compromised. It's only after the project baseline has been firmly established that the PM can start to manage changes off that baseline and determine the schedule, cost, or performance impacts of proposed project elements that weren't reflected in the original baseline.

It goes without saying (or maybe it doesn't) that we're talking about the baseline we all saw, reviewed, and signed off on. Without this widely communicated baseline, we can expect to be part of an uncomfortable conversation like this:

Stakeholder: We're looking forward to having that debt-forecasting ability we talked about in the new system.

PM: Well, I know it was discussed, but don't you recall that debt forecasting wasn't in our scope for planning? To include it, we'll have to put in a change request.

Stakeholder: Change request? That wasn't my understanding—I thought that debt forecasting was part of what we agreed to for the base system. There shouldn't be any additional cost or schedule impact for something that was in the base system, should there?

The baseline is, to use the biblical term, the "rock and foundation" off which we assess change. It's our starting point for schedule, for budget, and for performance. Without it, the PM doesn't have any "change-control control." Though saying yes or no to changes is the project sponsor's job, a PM with a baseline can say with confidence, "We'll certainly take a look at that change from the baseline and tell you what it means to the project schedule, budget, or performance."

b. **Actuals.** At each of the project milestones, how do our actual schedule, actual cost, and actual performance line up with where we expected to be?

c. **Forecasts.** Based on where we are for schedule, cost, and performance at each milestone, what is our forecast for schedule, costs, and performance at each milestone in the future?

This three-by-three reporting gives us the first nine of our 11 reporting elements:

1a. Schedule baseline

1b. Schedule actuals against planned schedule at each milestone

1c. Schedule forecast based on actuals to date

2a. Cost baseline

2b. Cost actuals against budgeted spending at each milestone

2c. Cost forecast based on spending to date

3a. Performance baseline

3b. Performance actuals against expected performance at each milestone

3c. Performance forecast based on actual performance to date.

The last two of the 11 reporting elements are:

• The project priority triangle at the current date

• The project risk register and how it lines up with the schedule.

Presented together, these 11 elements make up what a client called the GPS, or global positioning system, project status report. The client explained, "This [report] is like the GPS I carry when I'm hiking: It reminds me of where I'd planned to go and where I've come from (the *baseline*), where I am at any milestone in relation to my starting point (the *actuals*), and where I am in relation to my ultimate destination (the *forecasts*)." I liked the idea so much, I stole the name. Here's what a GPS contains:

1a. *Schedule baseline.* This is simply a matter of putting the existing 3D schedule on a 45-degree angle. The 3D represents the "straight line" through our project. Schedule actuals that are early or late will appear off the straight line (see Figure 23.1).

In Figure 23.1, the *x*-axis represents the weeks that have elapsed since the beginning of the project; the milestones along the 3D schedule line up with the weeks as we progress. If we planned

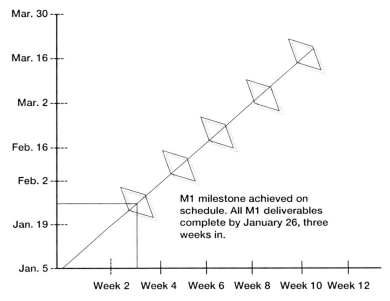

Figure 23.1 GPS: Schedule Baseline

to achieve our first milestone (M0) three weeks into the project, for example, the milestone diamond would line up above the three-week mark.

The *y*-axis represents actual calendar dates. Assuming a project start date (meaning the start of the execution phase) of January 5, 2009, three weeks from the start date would be January 26, so the milestone diamond would line up across from the 26th.

> **1b.** *Schedule actuals against planned schedule at each milestone.* This is where we report our actual dates against our plan.

We're right on schedule. If we made our first three-week milestone—that is, we delivered all our planned M1 deliverables on January 26—we would report that we were on track with schedule by filling in the actuals diamond on the 45-degree line and filling in a solid line up to that milestone, as shown in Figure 23.2. We're

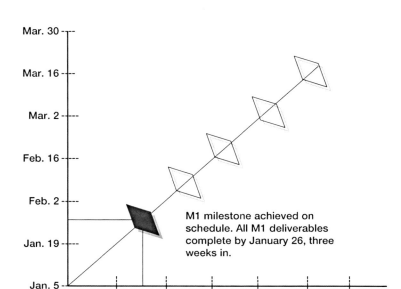

Figure 23.2 GPS: Schedule Baseline – On Schedule

reporting that, up to the first milestone, we're on track with our baseline schedule expectations.

We're running late. If, on the other hand, we *didn't* complete all of our expected three-week milestone deliverables, we'd need to report the date that we actually *did* complete these deliverables. Let's say we delivered the last of our milestone 1 deliverables one week late, on February 2. Our schedule tracking would look like Figure 23.3.

The achievement of any milestone—delivering all of the deliverables planned for that milestone—late will mean that the actuals diamond is recorded *above* the baseline, a clear and unequivocal communication of our late progress against our baseline schedule. Note that we're "claiming" the three-week milestone on the *x*-axis, but we didn't complete it on time, so our actuals diamond is reported *higher* on the *y*-axis, across from February 2, our actual completion date.

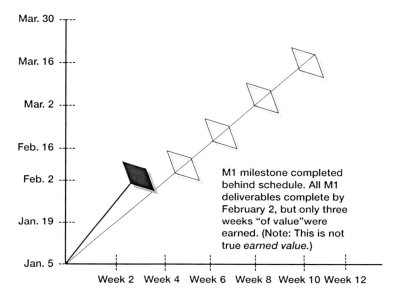

Figure 23.3 GPS: Schedule Baseline – Behind Schedule

We're ahead of schedule. If we delivered all of our expected three-week milestone deliverables *early*, we'd need to report the date that we completed all these deliverables. Let's say we delivered the last of our milestone 1 deliverables one week early, on January 19. Our schedule tracking would look like Figure 23.4:

The achievement of any milestone early will mean that the actuals diamond shows up below the baseline, a clear communication of our progress against our baseline schedule. Note that we're "claiming" the three-week milestone on the *x*-axis, but we completed it early, so our actuals diamond is reported *lower* on the *y*-axis, across from January 19, our actual completion date.

1c. *Schedule forecast based on actuals to date.* Based on where we are on the schedule and what we know to date, what are we forecasting for the schedule going forward? One of the project GPS's best features is that it allows teams to look forward.

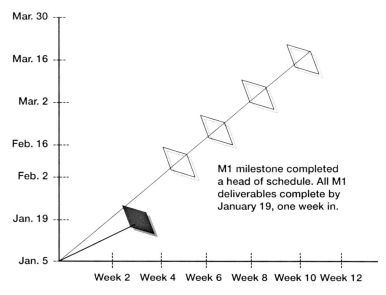

Figure 23.4 GPS: Schedule Baseline – Ahead of Schedule

Forecasting on schedule. If we're on schedule to date, our forecast should show that, all things being equal and assuming no changes, we'll finish in line with our baseline plan and schedule, as shown in Figure 23.5. Note the schedule forecast out to the end of the project, right on top of our baseline; we're right where we planned to be at the most recent reporting milestone.

Forecasting a late finish. If we're reporting that we're *behind* schedule at the most recent reporting milestone, we should show the impact on our end date. Remember that the 3D baseline schedule is a "when-does-it-have-to-be-finished-without-push-ing-out-the-end-date?" planning vehicle, on which we indicate the last date that deliverables can be completed without having an effect on the end date—a critical path through the project, if you will. There isn't any slack in our plan, and we haven't built in any contingency. This means that if we're running one week late at our first reporting milestone, we should expect to end our project at least a week late as well, as shown in Figure 23.6.

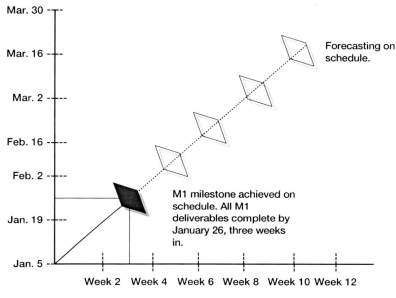

Figure 23.5 GPS: Schedule Baseline – Forecasting on Schedule

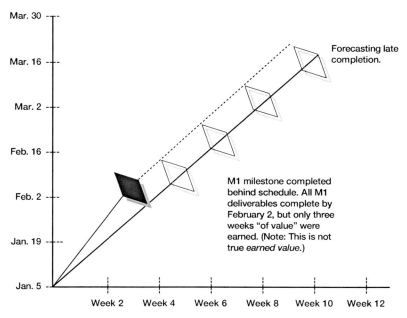

Figure 23.6 GPS: Schedule Baseline – Forecasting Late Completion

We may be able to fix that by adding resources or reducing our performance expectations (scope or quality), but we also know that the changes necessary to put us back on track will need to be accompanied by a change order—we would need to increase costs or reduce performance, after all—as part of our disciplined change-management process.

What we *shouldn't* do is just assume that we'll catch up. Late projects tend to get later; I haven't yet seen compelling evidence that work speeds up on projects over time. Telling your sponsor that you'll catch up is like saying, "We really did have some slack hidden in the project, although we didn't show it to you in the plan, and we hope to use that to catch up." Assuming you'll catch up because you're "coming up the learning curve" is even worse. A better idea? Be conservative and assume that you'll proceed per what your record to date is telling you. If you're two weeks behind now, without any changes to the budget or performance (scope and quality) expectations, you can expect to finish your project at least two weeks late, too.

Forecasting an early finish. If we're reporting that we're ahead of schedule at the most recent reporting milestone, we should show that anticipated impact, too. Does being a week ahead of schedule now mean we expect to finish the project a week early? Our forecast would look like Figure 23.7.

Reporting ahead of schedule, under budget, or both brings up an interesting question. If we're running ahead of schedule, should we be willing to advance the project end date—in other words, should we give up the time that it doesn't look like we'll need?

The same question applies to budget: If we're under budget but still making our schedule and delivering all our deliverables per our baseline plan, should we be willing to give back part of the budget when it becomes evident that we're underspending?

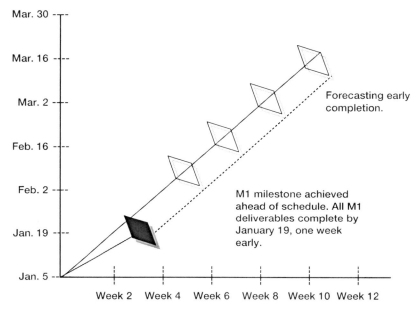

Figure 23.7 GPS: Schedule Baseline – Forecasting Early Completion

Most PMs are, to say the least, reluctant to give back schedule or budget, especially based on actuals up to the early milestones. If they're fortunate enough to be ahead of schedule, under budget, or both, the temptation to hold the extra time or budget in reserve is a strong one and understandable. A word of caution here: If you're running a true 3D schedule, you're operating under these conditions:

- Milestones have been set at the latest possible date they can be without affecting the end date.
- You've been telling people constantly about your no-slack, no-contingency policy and reminding them that if they're late with a deliverable at a milestone, all project dates following will get pushed back too, per the critical path.

Under these conditions—making milestones early or being under budget, assuming all expected deliverables have been delivered—a savvy sponsor or management team may well ask you to give back some of your schedule or budget: "You've told us that you're running a tight plan without slack or contingency, and we can see that. We can also see that at the third project milestone, you're three weeks ahead of schedule—that's really good news. You've made all your deliverables, and on top of that, you're $100,000 under budget. We also know that if you were over budget, you'd likely be here with a change request asking for additional funding. Shouldn't we, therefore, ask you to do a change request to move the project end date up by three weeks and take a hundred thousand out of the budget?"

Think about it, and be prepared to respond.

Drop dead date scheduling and reporting cuts both ways: Reporting against a 3D and an associated budget makes it abundantly clear where and when the project will need extra time and extra money, but it also will be obvious when you may need *less* time and *less* money, based on actuals to date.

> **2a. Cost baseline.** This one works much the same way as the schedule baseline, except that this baseline isn't a straight line. The idea is to show spending plans milestone by milestone as you progress—an indication of how much you expect to be burning, and how much you'll be needing, at every milestone.

If cash flow forecasting is important to your organization or to your client, the treasury and finance people will love you for using a project GPS; knowing how much the project will need on a milestone-by-milestone basis makes it easier for them to do their cash flow planning.

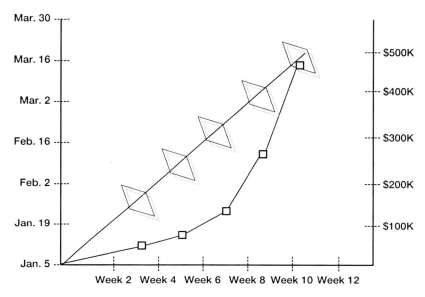

Figure 23.8 Typical Spending Baseline

When you lay out your budget baseline, you'll probably see some version of the typical project S curve—lower spending as you ramp up, a quick climb in costs as the team comes online or as you acquire the expensive assets you need to proceed, then a slowdown in spending as you head toward the end. Figure 23.8 shows a typical spending baseline for an IT project.

Note the checkpoints in Figures 23.9–23.21 and that they're set at early milestones in this example so that the project team and sponsor have the chance to review progress *before* major commitments are made, before the S curve heads north quickly, before the expensive consulting contracts are signed, and before the project team commits to the expensive capital equipment.

2b. *Cost actuals against budgeted spending.*

2c. *Cost forecast based on spending to date.*

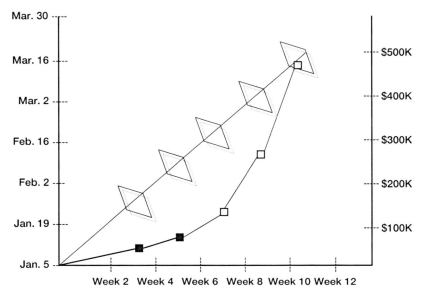

Figure 23.9 Spending Baseline – Actual Spending on Track

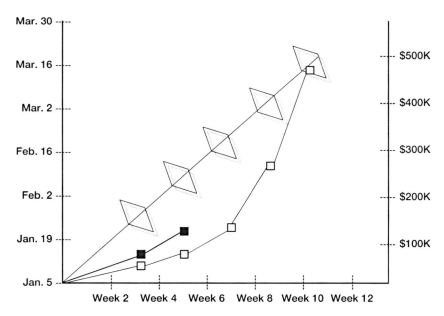

Figure 23.10 Spending Baseline – Actual Spending over Budget

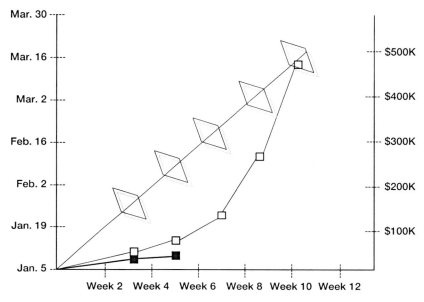

Figure 23.11 Spending Baseline – Actual Spending under Budget

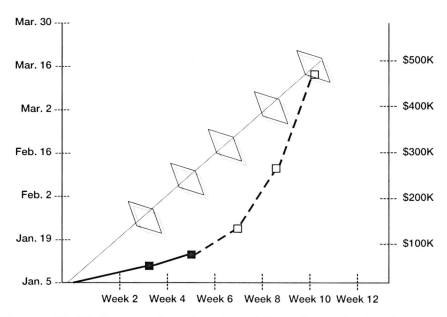

Figure 23.12 Forecast Based on Actual Spending – On Track

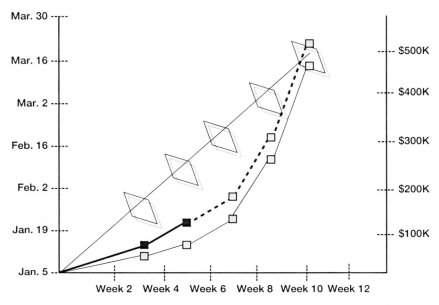

Figure 23.13 Forecast Based on Actual Spending – Over Budget

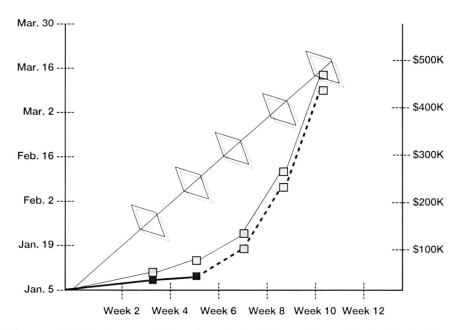

Figure 23.14 Forecast Based on Actual Spending – Under Budget

1. Reduce average call-handling time from four minutes per call to less than two minutes.

2. Reduce the call-handling staff by 30 percent.

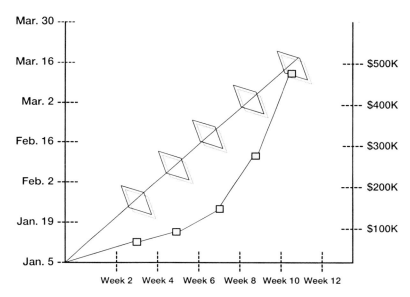

Figure 23.15 Project Performance Baseline

3a. Performance baseline.

3b. Performance actuals against expected performance at each milestone.

3c. Performance forecast based on actual performance to date.

So now we've looked at the first nine of our 11 reporting elements, including the schedule, cost, and performance baselines, actuals, and forecasts. What about the last two of the 11 reporting elements, the project triangle at the current date and the project risk register?

The project priority triangle in the GPS. The GPS also indicates your dominant priority at the time of reporting. Priori-

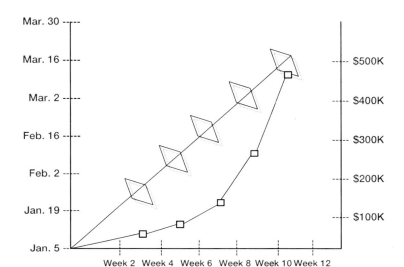

1. *Reduce average call-handling time from four minutes per call to less than two minutes.*

2. *Reduce the number of calls by 30 percent.*

Figure 23.16 Performance Expectations at Milestone 2

ties can change over the course of project performance; management may direct a team to put more emphasis on schedule, cost, or performance at any given time. The priority triangle on the GPS tells all readers how they can expect the PM to act in light of changes.

For example, maybe commodity prices have fallen and your mining client is now very concerned about cost control, certainly more than it was when the project started, when speed was the priority. I'd expect to see the triangle marked to reflect this revised priority and the PM to be managing accordingly. They may consider accommodating a change (and making a change request) that slows the project down a bit, if that would help keep costs in line, or they may suggest a change that would

1. Reduce average call-handling time from four minutes per call to less than two minutes.

2. Reduce the call-handling staff by 30 percent.

Call-handling time indicators show the average call time is lower than expected at Milestone 2.

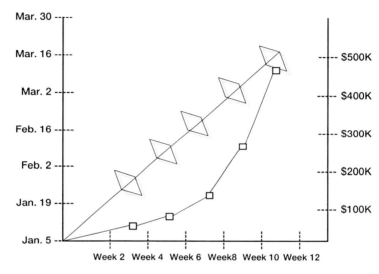

Figure 23.17 Performance Actuals – Average Call-Handling Time

affect performance, a reduction in scope or quality. I wouldn't expect the PM, in this case, to submit a change request that would increase costs.

Perhaps your client, a financial institution, has a regulatory compliance project that must be completed by a certain date per new legislation. In this case, I would expect to see an X marking *duration* in the priority triangle, signaling that although all control elements are important, making the date is the most important. The PM would try to accommodate the need for punctuality by submitting a change request that means spending a little more money, if this spending (on extra staff, maybe, or overtime) could help hold the end date. Alternatively, the PM could compromise performance.

1. *Reduce average call-handling time from four minutes per call to less than two minutes.*

2. *Reduce the call-handling staff by 30 percent.*

Indicators at Milestone 2 suggest the call-handling staff could be reduced by more than 30 percent.

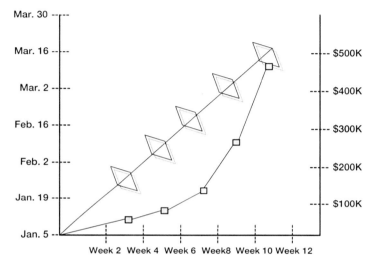

Figure 23.18 Performance Actuals – Call-Handling Staff

In either of these scenarios, I'd expect the behavior of the PM to be in line with the priorities indicated on the priority triangle as displayed in the GPS. For example, spending a little more money to stay on schedule is consistent with the direction provided by the priority triangle in Figure 23.22.

The risk schedule in the GPS, as lined up against the project schedule. The intention here is to show the reader when project risks are alive and the periods during which the project team will be managing those major risks. Determining the risks the team expects to deal with and how it will mitigate and manage them is important, but putting those risks in the context of the project schedule and spending plans is even more important. When reviewing progress, everyone reading the GPS should consider the status of project risks at every reporting point (see Figure 23.23).

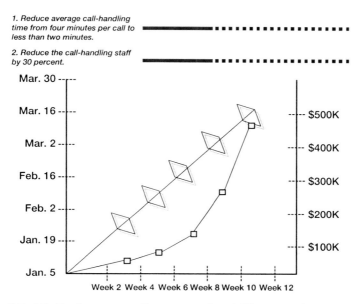

Figure 23.19 Performance Forecast after Milestone 2

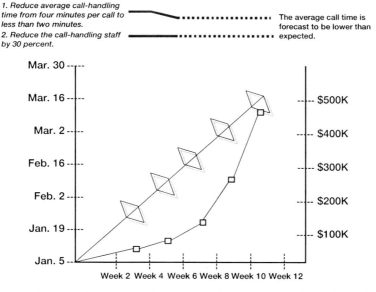

Figure 23.20 Performance Forecast – Average Call-Handling Time

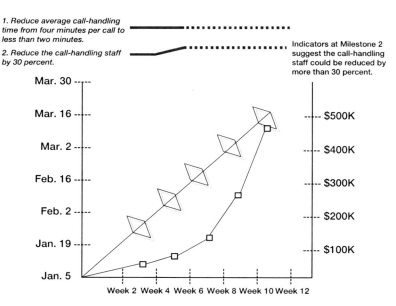

Figure 23.21 Performance Forecast – Call-Handling Staff

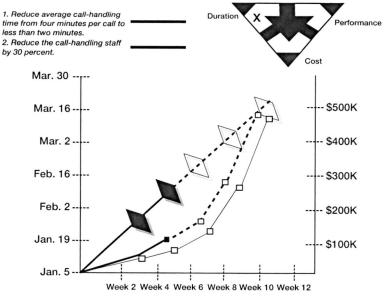

Figure 23.22 Managing Consistently with the Priority Triangle

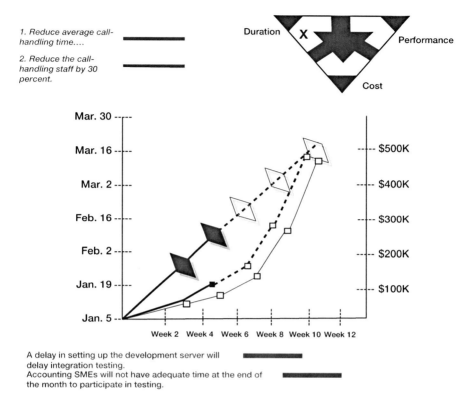

Figure 23.23 The Risk Schedule in the GPS

CHAPTER 24

READING THIS KIND OF PROJECT REPORTING

Better project reporting isn't just good for the PM. In fact, it's probably less about providing better information for the PM (who probably knows what's *really* going on in the project anyway, clear reporting or not) and more for the consumers of project reporting—the sponsors and other stakeholders who would otherwise have to sift through a combination of anecdotal updates and the traditional status reporting they usually get. One of the greatest benefits of improved project reporting is that well-executed reports help readers understand what they're seeing and, more important, the implications of what they're seeing.

Although the GPS goes a long way toward providing objectivity and clarity in project reporting, improved reporting really starts to take root in an organization when I get to spend time with the people who'll be reading the reports. Aside from reviewing reporting mechanics with project sponsors and executives (the PM should probably be present, too), I remind them that they should always be looking for (demanding?) consistency, clarity, and objectivity, and I guide them through sample reporting scenarios and the kinds of questions they should be asking—questions that will make them even better consumers of project reporting. Questions such as:

What if the Project Team Is Reporting that It's on Schedule for all of Its Deliverables, but It Has Overspent Its Budget?

Management should want to know why this is. Did the team have to put in overtime (which costs extra) to make the deliverables to date? If so, should they expect that pattern to continue? Are the project reports forecasting a continuing cost overrun to keep deliverables on schedule?

If the project team says that it expects spending to come back in line as the project progresses, management should ask how the team plans to do this. Remember, if a team is over budget on the deliverables it has delivered to date, it will have to deliver the rest of the deliverables *under budget* to come back to the budget baseline (see Figure 24.1).

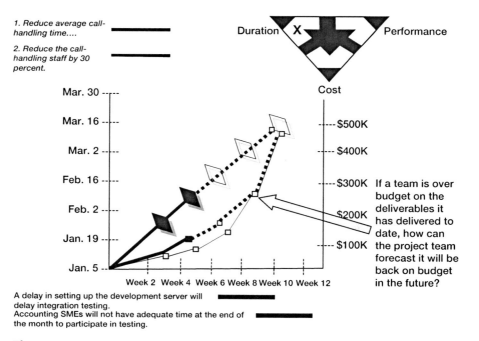

Figure 24.1 On Schedule, But over Budget

What if the Team Is Reporting that It's behind Schedule, but the "Good News" Is that It Is under Budget?

In and of itself, this information makes sense; the team hasn't delivered as much as it planned to, so it hasn't spent as much as it planned, either. But what if the sponsor prioritizes schedule, as reflected in the project priority triangle, over budget? Per the triangle, which of the three disciplines—schedule, cost, or performance—is the most important? And is the team behaving/managing the project in a manner consistent with that indicated by the priority triangle?

In a case like this, I suggest that the sponsor remind the project team of the priorities they've all agreed to, according to the priority triangle:

> We all agreed that schedule is the priority on this project. Is there a way that we can spend some more of the budget— we are under budget, after all—to catch up? If we agreed that staying on schedule is even more important than the budget, why would we be pleased about an underspend when we're running behind schedule?

There may, in fact, be a good reason for this turn of events; maybe what's running behind can't be sped up with money. But it's a good and insightful question to ask, and one that will emerge naturally with this kind of project reporting.

Should Project Checkpoints and Potential Off-ramps Be set before Teams Make Major Commitments of Dollars and Resources?

We should be looking for checkpoints and off-ramps that'll allow us take appropriate action while there's still time to positively affect outcomes. Setting off-ramps (circumstances under which it would make sense to stop a project) is almost always a good idea, but not if the first time the off-ramps turn up is after 80 percent of the budget is gone and 75 percent of the schedule has passed (see Figure 24.2). No one's going to thank the PM for identifying an off-ramp condition at that late point.

I encourage the team to establish, and management to look for, checkpoints and off-ramps that are set as early as possible, as soon as good information about the health of the project first becomes available—information that will help with forecasting the future.

Remember that spending S curve? Wherever possible, we want checkpoints and off-ramps to be set *before* the S curve heads up

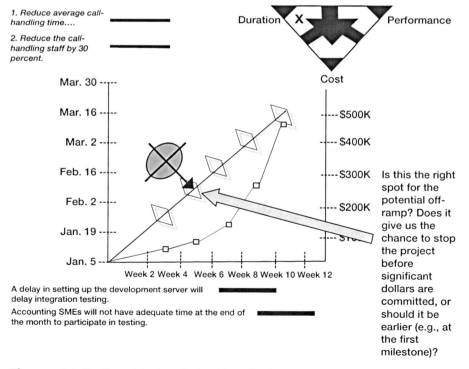

Figure 24.2 Considering Potential Off-Ramps

sharply, so that we can all take a hard look at how the project is doing *before* we make the commitments that will rapidly increase our burn rate.

Stopping a project that looks like it will be unsuccessful *before* the commitment of big dollars and large numbers of resources is smart management; doing the same after most of the budget has been spent isn't nearly as smart. The best project-hosting organizations tend to be the ones that prune unsuccessful projects early. Stopping projects that don't look like they'll be a success isn't a failure, it's good management, and early off-ramps support good management.

How can the Risk Schedule Affect Our View of how a Project Is Progressing?

The risk schedule adds a layer of context and intelligence to GPS reporting, and project reporting should be viewed in light of it. The project team, for example, may be reporting that it is a little behind schedule, but team members are certain that "with a few changes, we'll get back on track." A smart sponsor would do well to take a close look at the risk schedule when considering this information. If the project team is mostly past the big risks on the project—that is, the high-impact, high-probability risks—the sponsor and other readers might take what the team is saying at face value. If the big concerns regarding project risk, for example, were about uncertainty in estimates and potential delays in code development, but the team is already past them and into testing, a small delay at this reporting point may not reflect a serious concern.

What if, on the other hand, a big risk window is still ahead of the team? What if the team is behind schedule in analysis and design, for example, and the big development risks are still in the future? In this case, the sponsor and other stakeholders may want to take a harder look at progress to date and the project's prospects for the future. If the team is behind schedule now, and it hasn't even reached the high-risk part of the project, what makes us think that it's not going to fall even further behind?

Reporting Frequency? That Depends

Status reports that turn up every week when there's been no material change of interest to the reader waste the PM's time, and worse, they tend to bore readers. If readers get used to seeing an almost entirely unchanged status report come across their desks every week, they are going to stop looking at it—and that's a bad thing when the report does include important information.

In general, status reports should be produced at every project milestone (milestones representing major progress points in the project) or more frequently:

- At the request of the project sponsor or any other major stakeholder
- If milestones are more than a month apart.

In any case, the frequency of reporting should be discussed, and agreed to, with the project sponsor in advance. It may make sense to report more frequently during particularly active (or risky, or deliverable-heavy, or leading-up-to-an-off-ramp) periods in the project.

It does make sense to share information through reporting when things are changing and when new and important information about the project becomes available. Readers need to know what's going on ahead of important decisions. It doesn't make sense to mechanically crank out a status report just because it's time to put one out.

FINAL THOUGHTS

When I sit down with clients to talk about improving their overall project management capabilities, their first question is usually: "Where do we start?" I think my answer surprises them. "Start where all the pros start their projects," I say. "Start at the end." By that I mean start by improving how you close out projects and what you learn from them, before you tackle anything else.

In fact, I'd suggest that you work on improvements to your project management practices in this order:

1. Project closeouts and lessons learned

2. Strategic portfolio management

3. Effective project planning

4. Project management

Why closeouts and lessons learned first? Because your organization is already in the projects business—the very least you can do is learn something from the projects you've finished by capturing and formalizing lessons learned and then deliberately and explicitly applying those lessons to future projects.

It's down to this: If deliverable number one in your project plan *isn't* a review of previous project closeout and lessons learned reports, your project planning is deficient. If you're not capturing lessons from completed projects and ensuring that your project teams are applying those lessons to every subsequent project, your organization is losing valuable information every day.

Next? Become good at selecting projects, more formally called *strategic portfolio management.* Before planning and managing projects well, you've got to be sure you're choosing the right set of projects to manage. There's nothing worse than planning and managing the wrong set of projects—projects that don't explicitly align with your organization's strategies and goals.

Once the right set of projects are chosen, *then* comes the project planning part, the important stuff covered in this book.

Last (and least) comes "basic" project management itself. In fact, project *management,* in the strict sense of the word, is fairly straightforward—it's really a matter of *managing to the plan,* managing the impact of changes as they occur, staying close to the project stakeholder community, and ensuring that what the project delivers lines up with the reasons why the project was chosen in the first place. Sure, project *management* is important, but it's not as important as the planning that precedes it.

Think about that the next time you refer to yourself as a project *manager*—the role you're playing is so much more than just managing.

Good luck.

INDEX

Integrated Cost and Schedule Control in Project Management, Second Edition
Ursula Kuehn, PMP

Building on the solid foundation of the first edition, this updated second edition includes new material on project planning in the federal government, integrated baseline reviews (IBRs), federal requirements for an ANSI/EIA-748 compliant earned value management system, and federal requirements for contract performance reports (CPRs). This book continues to offer a practical approach that is accessible to project managers at all levels. The step-by-step presentation, numerous case studies, and instructive examples give practitioners relevant material they can put to use immediately.

ISBN 978-1-56726-296-4 ■ Product Code B964 ■ 319 pages

Project Team Dynamics: Enhancing Performance, Improving Results
Lisa DiTullio

Companies that embrace the power of collaboration realize that the best way to solve complex problems is to build cohesive teams made up of members with different skills and expertise. Getting teams to work productively is at the heart of project management. Developing the structure for teams to work at a high level of efficiency and effectiveness is at the heart of this book. Lisa DiTullio clearly outlines methods for creating and implementing a framework to deal with the inevitable difficulties that any team will encounter. With examples drawn from contemporary project management, she demonstrates the effectiveness of this straightforward approach and the risks of not building a strong team culture.

ISBN 978-1-56726-290-2 ■ Product Code B902 ■ 179 pages

Project Management Fundamentals: Key Concepts and Methodology, Second Edition
Gregory Haugan, PhD, PMP

To achieve success in any endeavor, you need to understand the fundamental aspects of that endeavor. To achieve success in project management, you should start with this completely revised edition that offers new project managers a solid foundation in the basics of the discipline. Using a step-by-step approach and conventional project management terminology, *Project Management Fundamentals* is a commonsense guide that focuses on how essential project management methods, tools, and techniques can be put into practice immediately.

ISBN 978-1-56726-281-0 ■ Product Code B810 ■ 380 pages

Interpersonal Skills for Portfolio, Program, and Project Managers
Ginger Levin, DPA, PMP, PgMP

Any formula for management success must include a high level of interpersonal skills. The growing complexity of portfolios, programs, and projects, as well as the increasing number and geographic dispersion of stakeholders, makes a manager's interpersonal skills critical. The frequency and variety of interpersonal interactions and the pressure to execute portfolios, programs, and projects successfully while ensuring customer satisfaction have never been greater. This book offers practical and proven tools and methods you can use to develop your interpersonal skills and meet the challenges of today's competitive professional environment.

ISBN 978-1-56726-288-9 ■ Product Code B889 ■ 286 pages

Organizational Project Management: Linking Strategy and Projects
Edited by Rosemary Hossenlopp, PMP

Organizational project management (OPM) aligns project deliverables with strategy. Understanding this emerging process is essential for all stakeholders, from the corporate sponsor to project team members. OPM is a valuable new tool that can enhance your organization's successful execution of projects in alignment with strategic priorities. Under the editorship of Rosemary Hossenlopp, PMP, ten contributors from around the globe, representing a wide variety of industries, offer valuable insights on how OPM can give any organization the competitive edge.

ISBN 978-1-56726-282-7 ■ Product Code B827 ■ 193 pages

Achieving Project Management Success in the Federal Government
Jonathan Weinstein, PMP, and Timothy Jaques, PMP

The authors offer a realistic cross section of the project management discipline in the largest single enterprise in the world—the U.S. federal government. Based on research and interviews with a wide variety of project managers who shared their lessons learned and advice, this book offers practical guidance and insights to federal leaders, project team members, and others involved with project management in the government.

ISBN 978-1-56726-275-9 ■ Product Code B759 ■ 304 pages

Delivering Project Excellence with the Statement of Work, Second Edition
Michael G. Martin, PMP

This second edition builds on the foundation of the first edition with a comprehensive yet succinct description of how to develop and apply the statement of work (SOW) to manage projects effectively. With updates throughout and an entirely new chapter on the use and application of the statement of objectives, this book continues to serve as a practical guide for project managers and team members. The new edition includes coverage of project management issues related to the federal government such as updated FAR guidance on drafting a quality SOW and a discussion of legal considerations related to the SOW.

ISBN 978-1-56726-257-5 ■ Product Code B575 ■ 380 pages

The 77 Deadly Sins of Project Management
Management Concepts

Projects can be **negatively** impacted by common "sins" that hinder, stall, or throw the project off track. *The 77 Deadly Sins of Project Management* helps you better understand how to execute projects by providing individual anecdotes and case studies of the project management sins described by experts in the field.

SBN 978-1-56726-246-9 ■ Product Code B777 ■ 357 pages